GO
GENTLE
INTO
THE
NIGHT

Books by C. L. Sulzberger

C. L. SULZ

BERGER

GO
GENTLE
INTO
THE
NIGHT

PRENTICE-HALL, INC., *Englewood Cliffs, N.J.*

Design by Linda Huber

Go Gentle Into the Night by C. L. Sulzberger
Printed in the United States of America
Prentice-Hall International, Inc., London
Prentice-Hall of Australia, Pty. Ltd., Sydney
Prentice-Hall of Canada, Ltd., Toronto
Prentice-Hall of India Private Ltd., New Delhi
Prentice-Hall of Japan, Inc., Tokyo

10 9 8 7 6 5 4 3 2 1

Library of Congress Cataloging in Publication Data
Sulzberger, Cyrus Leo
    Go gentle into the night.
    Includes index.
        1. Prayer.   2. Prayers.   3. Religion.
4. Death.   5. Sulzberger, Cyrus Leo
I. Title.
BL560.S94   242   75-42344
ISBN 0-13-357293-5

CONTENTS

In memory of Chip Bohlen

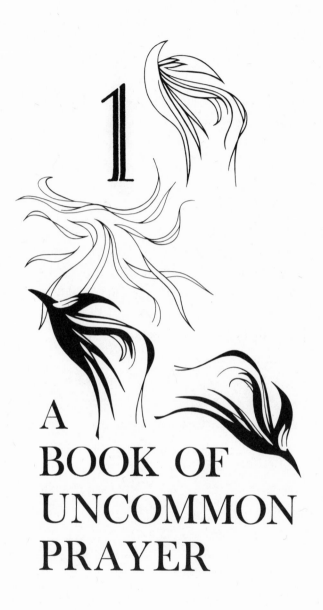

1

A
BOOK OF
UNCOMMON
PRAYER

When I first began to write this, the product of many years of reflection, I called it (as the first chapter is now known) "A Book of Uncommon Prayer." The reason for such a title, or if you will, mistitle, is that the prayers included in my anthology of preferences are often most uncommon in terms of the desire they express or the words in which they are couched; also, some of them would not ordinarily even be known or defined as prayers.

Yet the pleas, the dreams herein contained, even if not to be categorized under the word normally understood with reference to praying, cannot otherwise be listed. The subjects discussed in these yearnings are all-embracing, and while each is not addressed to divinity, this volume is primarily about men and their own relationship to the immortal, not about God as such.

As a journalist, all my life my business has been mankind: the generals, statesmen, presidents, prelates, the dunces and diplomats, the princesses and prostitutes, the captains and kings. How can anyone devoted to a trade so based on the persistence of inquiry ignore the innermost hopes and aspirations of our species?

All men may not acknowledge a god, above all the same god, but all are bound by common destiny. There is no choice in being born—against the most incredible mathematical odds that procreation will occur and will create. And there is great pain involved in the process of birth, for the subject

involved as well as the mother, although this pain
is always forgotten because the brain is too young
for memory. Likewise, there is no choice for those
born but to die. The event is inescapable and generally also dolorous. Yet that dolor likewise is not
remembered—nor the life expiring with it—amid
that state we know as death.

During the unremembered passage from pain
to pain, that agitated and electrifying period we
call life, the majority of human creatures share similar experiences of joy and sorrow, exuberance,
awe and love, combat and fear, despair and hope,
tranquility and turmoil. And when those experiences
are of the sad or negative variety, or when there is
a craving for benefit or merely an adoring of the
beautiful, most men have developed the habit of
praying in appreciation, or in fear, or in desire.
These expressions are often among the loveliest of
man's creations, uttered either directly or indirectly for
man's own solace on the all-too-brief road between the
poles of pain.

Since Cro-Magnon days a divinity of some
sort, either perceived by mankind's sapience, deliberately created in his own image, or inspired by
respect for what he cannot comprehend, is man's
primordial and primary object of special prayers
of reverence. For most people a divine auditor is
essential to psychological self-confidence. Thus
throughout the relatively brief period of recorded
time, prayer has become an approach to supra-

human deity in word or thought; and this custom has been reinforced and strengthened by centuries of tradition.

Theological compilations of virtually every formal sect or faith have their own more precise (and often more limited) definitions of prayer—what it is or should be, its recommended form and use. My feeling is that there should be no fixed limitations of scope. Appeals for aid or paeans to bliss need not always be connected to theology or the formalizations of any credo. Beauty, after all, is a religion in itself.

Prayer is an all-encompassing phenomenon. The only totally common experience to which such an appeal is not addressed (except in fancy, as by Virgil) is death itself. No one prays to death, to nothingness, only to the hope that it is but camouflage for another form of life.

With respect to that broad range of literary expression known as prayer, whether theistic, deistic, or poetic, I have spent more than four decades collecting selections that struck me as memorable or poignant. These are what I call "uncommon prayers," joined (regardless of individual credo) by the intrinsic quality of their content.

To a considerable extent, these uncommon prayers display the perspective of humanity, its dreams, its fears, its weaknesses and strengths: a complete panoply of man against the awesome background of his own imagination. Yet I recognize that to some people it may seem strange or even presumptuous that an atheist, which is my own anti-credo, should compile a book of prayers, especially since most of them are addressed to various divinities by faithful adherents.

Nevertheless, one does not have to believe in God to respect godliness. It is not necessary to accept theism or abstract ethic in order to admire the methodology of virtue. And prayers, inherently, are human truth. They expose that stark naked fellow, the soul.

Atheism is not necessarily intolerant as a non-belief. Indeed, I should think the contrary. I could never wish its loneliness and helplessness on anyone who has not himself found and trod the long, hard, solitary road of that abysmal state. What atheist would ever seek to proselytize others who, more fortunate, have confidence in a higher being, a divinely arranged order—or disorder?

Indeed, that anticredo to which I have condemned myself contains its own exquisite torture. Saint Thérèse of Lisieux so suspected shortly before her death in 1896:

> Darkness itself, borrowing the voice of the unbeliever, cries mockingly. . . . Hope on! . . . Hope on! . . . Look forward to death! It will give you, not what you hope for, but a night darker still, the night of utter nothingless!

And the dear girl (she was but twenty-three when she died) confided to her simple copybook:

> I tell Him that I am ready to shed my blood as a witness to my belief in Heaven. I tell Him that if He will

deign to open it for eternity to poor unbelievers, I am content to sacrifice during my life all joyous thoughts of the Home that awaits me.

It is one of history's curiosities that the first divinities conceived were things—like sun, moon, wind, fire—and that when humanity at last ventured to create a personal god to console itself, the first gods were women: Gaia, the Earth Mother; Inana; Astarte. Only centuries later was the sex of the Supreme Being altered; man asserted himself at all levels of thought. Moreover, God is always represented in the shape and race of those who, as it were, made Him. In East Asia His face is marked by the Mongol fold. In India He is brown. In the United States He is surely a WASP (White Anglo-Saxon Protestant), although the majority of the population no longer is; and even for Catholics and Jews, God would surely be a member of their country club.

Atheism does not preclude knowledge of and respect for religion or friendship with the most religious of one's fellows, even the theologians of our time. During my life I have been on close terms with priests, patriarchs, rabbis, Islamic muftis and philosophers, and Oriental prelates—some fascinating, some dour, some visionary, some pragmatic.

Over twenty years ago, with one of its military adherents, I visited the headquarters of the South Vietnamese sect of Cao Dai, a curious mélange of religion and private army. At that time Cao Dai ran a feudal state in an area around Tay Ninh, its holy city, near the Cambodian border. Its organization, then ruled by a theologian called the Superior (as they awaited opportunity to elect their next pope) included male and female priests and priestesses, bishops and cardinals.

Theirs, I must say, was a convincingly catholic belief derived from everywhere. On both sides of the cathedral were gaily painted pillars ornamented with flowers and with twisting serpents writhing above the white-clad priests and priestesses. Overhead were representations of demons bearing axes, and world maps bordered by slogans: "God and Humanity," "Love and Justice."

The symbol of Cao Dai was (and is) a human eye. Its three principal saints are Victor Hugo, Sun Yat-sen, and a Vietnamese named Nguyen Binh Khiem. They were then planning to canonize Winston Churchill when he became eligible—by dying. Incense burned at the altar in honor of Cao Dai, Buddha, Christ, Confucius, and Lao-tse.

So strange and unfamiliar a medley tends, for Westerners, to obscure the credo's inner value. Yet other better-known, more conventional and spiritual faiths also contain a broad range of unexpected temporal problems that sometimes complicate thought, reflection, and life.

I was introduced quite early to the intramural rivalries for God's domain of vying sects which pretend to control heavenly access. In early 1942, during the Second World War, when I came down to the Middle East from Moscow in order to marry my fiancée, then Marina Lada, a lovely Greek (and Greek Orthodox) girl, I was horrified to discover that this conventionally moral project had become an occasion for priestly quarrels.

Marina was staying in Jerusalem with Shan Sedgwick, her American uncle then a correspondent with the tiny British Tenth Army, which had occupied southern Iran and driven the Vichy French from Syria and Lebanon. The Holy City was at that time capital of Britain's Palestine Mandate, a territory ruled by London in the name of a moribund League of Nations.

Shan, my good friend, made inquiries and soon discovered that only British subjects including neither Marina nor myself could be wedded in a civil—not clerical—ceremony. Refusing to be nonplussed, he reckoned there would be no difficulty since Jerusalem was a religious center without equal, boasting numerous patriarchs, bishops, rabbis, mullahs, and simple Protestant pastors.

However, the Greek patriarch assured Marina, whom he knew well, that it was beyond his powers to arrange a swift linkup between a virtuous Greek Orthodox girl and a heathen like myself. The Grand Rabbi told Shan and his niece it would indeed be agreeable to him, but Marina would first have to learn Hebrew, convert to the Jewish faith, and then persuade a qualified ecclesiastical board that she had changed religions out of belief, not out of love. When Sedgwick, in a moment of despair, murmured the possibility of Islam, Marina put her foot down. "I refuse to be blacked out for the rest of my life," she said, thinking of the veiled ladies one saw those days in Jerusalem's Arab quarter.

Finally the persistent and loyal Sedgwick discovered an American Scottish-Presbyterian clergyman named Dr. Scherer who was serving as a chaplain to the British forces in the Lebanon, administered in theory by Free France. Scherer agreed to do the job. Promptly after my arrival, he married us with the assistance of Bill Porter, a young Catholic diplomat, later a distinguished U. S. ambassador, who agreed to certify the mundane legality of the affair. Even Scherer, however, had his moment of doubt.

A tall, pleasant-faced man wearing British uniform beneath his cassock, he invited Marina and me into his study before the ceremony to explain his difficulties in preparing a proper service because the only formula he knew was Presbyterian. He intended, with our approval, to preface this with a special apologia: "Dear God. I know I am departing from custom and, as it were, stepping out of my bailiwick today as I join these two young people in holy wedlock. But You are undoubtedly aware of all the trouble that exists nowadays on earth. I can only assure You their two hearts beat as one."

And so, by these complicated means, an American atheist wedded a Greek Orthodox with a Roman Catholic witness in a service performed by a Presbyterian minister wearing British uniform in Free France. We are, thirty-four years later, still married.

Imagine the difficulties of severing that theological Gordian knot!

Of various clergymen I have known through the years, several still come to mind. One was Dr. Judah Magnes, an American rabbi living in Mandated Palestine, who always argued in favor of a joint Arab-Jewish state rather than a Zionist country such as Israel was to become. His views, as the reader can imagine, were unpopular with virtually all the Jewish organizations then feverishly working underground to oust both British and Arabs from the Holy Land. Both that practical but now discarded cause and Magnes himself have long since been dead.

The church of Islam is far less formally organized than most monotheistic creeds. Almost thirty years ago I asked Saudi Arabia's proto-king, Abdul Aziz Ibn Saud, that remarkable sovereign of Mecca and conservative leader of the Arabs, if he thought the time had come to revive the ancient institution of the caliphate, abolished together with the sultanate in Turkey after Mustapha Kemal's revolution.

The caliph had been the apex of Islam's loose priestly structure. But aged Ibn Saud, a massive man who spoke and looked like some imposing Old Testament prophet, said he saw no need for that office's restoration, "and consequently I do not consider either myself or anyone else as a candidate."

In the absence of a caliphate, probably the most revered figure in the Moslem world is the rector of Al Azhar, Cairo's theological university and center for devout students from all over Islam. Sheikh Mahmoud Shaltout, a relatively recent holder of that post, once explained to me, "There is no authority in Islam save for the Koran itself. There are some leaders such as the rectors of Al Azhar and other universities, but they have no authority in a clerical sense.

"In fact, the caliph never had any religious authority. This belongs to God alone, as revealed in the Koran. There is no single man or group above others in Islam; each man thinks for himself. Islam has no formal directing organization or clergy. Every individual is God's vice-gerent." (I remember thinking to myself at the time: how strange—Islam has God but no clergy; Buddhism has a clergy but no God.)

Nevertheless, the Moslem muftis play a considerable role in their religious society and often, also, have political influence. Of all with whom I have talked, by far the most romantically interesting was Ishan Babahan Ibn Abdul Majid Khan, mufti of Soviet Central Asia. I visited him in 1956 at his home in Tashkent, a city where he had been born in 1860. In other words, he was ninety-five years old and had been originally a subject of the independent Central Asian Khan of Kokand, then of the czar, and finally the commissars: a wisp of a man sitting up in a chair; dressed in flowered, black robe and flat, honey-colored turban; a straggly beard falling from his toothless jaw; a brown face, dull brown eyes, and a fierce hawk nose. Once he clearly had been a powerful heavy-chested man, now but small and shrunken.

He and his son, the acting mufti (Al Hafiz

Ghazi Zia-ud-Din Babahanov, a pleasant, Turkish-looking individual in tan robe and white turban), explained sadly how Islam had tumbled in the once-famous realm of Kokand. In 1917, when the Bolshevik revolution began, there had been three hundred mosques serving a population of six hundred thousand; now there were but eighteen for a million potential worshippers. "Allah Akbar, Ya Ho, Ya Hak," intoned the kneeling faithful in a diminutive white mosque not far away. But Allah's support is declining to the vanishing point in the USSR, whose official atheism, unlike mine, is sternly intolerant.

I have known two Greek prelates well. One was Athenagoras, Orthodox patriarch of Istanbul. For years he dominated the quarrelsome leaders of orthodoxy, as the first among bickering equals (much as the Catholic pope was originally supposed to be but a bishop with protocol priority before his church adopted the brilliant military organizational talents of the latter-day Romans).

Athenagoras, a huge man with carefully combed long gray beard, resembled Michaelangelo's Moses. He dwelt in modest circumstances in the Phanar quarter of Istanbul, last living symbol of the former Greek imperial rule in Constantinople. I shall never forget his saying sadly to me one day: "How can the spiritual world face conflict with the materialist world when it cannot agree with itself? Religion is behaving criminally. It is at war in Christendom."

The other Orthodox dignitary whom I saw frequently over the years was Archbishop Makarios III, long president of Cyprus but also ethnarch of the island's Greek community. His office, as head of an autocephalous branch of orthodoxy, permitted him three special privileges granted in the fifth century by the Byzantine Emperor Zeno: He could sign his name in red ink, wear a purple mantle, and carry an imperial scepter (instead of a bishop's staff) on ceremonial occasions.

Makarios ruled the world's largest theocracy (which Cyprus's lay government technically was) once the Dalai Lama had to flee Tibet. The pope's domain of Vatican City is infinitesimal by comparison; and the Imam who ruled Islamic Yemen has long been dispossessed. But when I asked the archbishop if, in his dual role, he thought there was conflict between that which was God's and that which was Caesar's, especially with respect to the Moslem Turkish-speaking citizens he governed, his reply was:

"No, there is no conflict of interest. . . . Perhaps there are some advantages to having an ecclesiastic as a ruler. There might also be some disadvantages; for example, it takes time away from normal religious duties, but I find it doesn't really interfere. And, after all, even in politics there is no different standard of right and wrong from that in religious life. What is right in the latter is also right in the former. Something cannot be both just and unjust. . . .

Religion teaches morality and morality should always be at the base of political life, as it should in all other aspects of life."

Alas, the Turkish citizens of Cyprus, imbued with the Turks' ancient prejudice against the warlike and politically minded priests of the Balkan Christian areas, never showed wholehearted acceptance of these views and remained deeply skeptical of the sincerity of the archbishop's statements.

It has been my fortune also to know reasonably well several Roman Catholic princes of the church. During World War II, I flew with my wife from Algiers to Cairo aboard a Dakota bearing Francis, Cardinal Spellman, then archbishop of New York, who was allowed to take the plane's controls. Later, when I wrote that he had thus become a true sky pilot (American slang for clergyman), the censor removed the phrase, for reasons known only to himself and God. In Benghazi, Libya, where we stopped for fuel at the airport littered with wrecked German transport aircraft, poor Spellman was persuaded with some embarrassment to use the one Junker whose toilet facilities were designated for "skirts." The rest of us (except my wife) queued up at what remained of another battered, swastikaed, winged latrine.

Pope Pius XII, the one pontiff with whom I was truly acquainted, was an interesting man who, after 1945, came in for what almost surely is an unfair amount of criticism because he didn't stop the conflict Hitler started and because he didn't do more

to save Europe's Jews from Nazi extermination.
In the immediate postwar years, when I had the
privilege of talking with him from time to time,
he was a thin old man with delicate hands, sharp
features, penetrating eyes, and an extraordinary
fascination for politics. He worried enormously
about each Italian local election. He could recite
voting statistics and probabilities quite as fluently as
that later Texas political seer and poll worshipper,
Lyndon B. Johnson.

Once I asked Pius why he was so uncompromis-
ingly anticommunist (a view that was toned down
by subsequent popes.) He said it was because there
could be no compromise between spiritualism and
materialism; that it was impossible for a good
Catholic to be at the same time a political communist
(an interpretation the Vatican also later altered).
On another occasion I inquired why he did not
practice what he preached, in this respect, and
seek to organize some kind of international "front"
of all monotheistic believers: Catholic, Protestant,
Moslem, Jewish, etc., in order to combat the "materialism" against whose threat he warned. He thought
a moment, then he suggested I pose this question
to his acting secretary of state, Monsignor Montini,
with whom he would arrange an appointment.

When I did just that, Montini (who eventually
became Pope Paul VI) explained with hesitation
that what I had by inference suggested was ex-
tremely difficult and delicate. The Church of Rome
considered itself to be the "only true Church."

Therefore it could not even implicitly acknowledge the viable theological existence of other sects. This, I may add, was before the days when John XXIII approached the concept of ecumenism.

Perhaps the most intellectually stimulating companion I had in Moscow during the first months of Hitler's Russian invasion in 1941 was Father Leopold Braun, an American Augustinian friar and maybe at that time the sole openly practicing Roman Catholic prelate in the Soviet Union. I stress "openly" because there was a little-known handful of secret practitioners—almost all in concentration camps. Several times, with Pope Pius, I discussed Braun, that doughty, belligerent champion of a faith I respected but did not share, a man unheard of by most of his priestly colleagues, but vastly esteemed by the Vatican.

With a chapel regularly raided by Stalin's secret police, a tiny congregation under steady menace, and a threadbare and Spartan existence guarded by a single, faithful, powerful black dog, his enemy was atheism—as represented by the personally hostile, antireligious, communist state. And yet, although he knew of my godless outlook, he tolerated me—for my outlook on other things, if not for my virtue.

In different circumstances, less artificially proscribed, one can imagine even more natural and uninhibited relationships between the God-fearing and the godless. Indeed, on learning that I was compiling this small anthology, my old friend Pax Kennedy, a Franciscan monk (Rev. Pacificus

Kennedy, O.F.M.), as tolerant as he is humane, worthy follower of the gentlest saint, called to my attention a book of "Prayers and Reflections by a Believer for a Skeptic" (*To Barbara With Love,* by a devout Catholic, Joan Bel-Geddes) which includes this admission:

> I can't get rid of my doubt, but I'm going to give God—at least temporarily—"the benefit of doubt" and see what happens.

She also counsels her skeptical sister, Barbara:

> I know there are many people who are convinced that God actually knows them and loves them and looks after them individually. If them, why not me too? Maybe they know something I don't.

This suggestion tends to confirm my suspicion: Only poets or gamblers, those fully aware of the odds, are naturally religious—as compared with those who acquire that characteristic. Moreover, since most humans are religious—virtually all, if one accepts the ideological concept that you don't require a god to pay respect to virtue—most humans must also be poets or gamblers, if not both. Beauty is truth—plus loser take nothing.

The idea that it is folly to take a chance, when maybe one could be wrong, lies at the heart of the Yezidi belief in the Middle East, that cradle of religion where the heavens seem somehow more exposed to man. The Yezidi worship the devil on the logical assumption that if God wins his contest with evil

he will be all-merciful, notwithstanding; but
would it not be wise to propitiate Satan, in case he
should win instead? For, let us face it, the bland,
confident universality of that lumbering Neapolitan mystic, St. Thomas Aquinas, has been
replaced by an era of agonizing doubts; nothing is
demonstrably certain today save acknowledgment
of infinity in terms of man's own unimportance
to anyone at all.

I fear Christianity's concept of God as love is not
nearly so general, even in that portion of the world
proclaiming itself Christian, as an atavistic fear
of the suprahuman which goes back as far as thought
itself. Such dread is easiest to trace in its devilish
aspect or what we would call demonology, a practice
by no means extinct.

The Yezidi creed, whose practicants are Kurdish
and call themselves Dasni, live in northern Iraq. Their
belief, although modified by contact with Christianity
and Islam, probably stems from the ancient Zoro-
astrian fire-worshipping sect. They calculate that
the devil is benevolent God's subordinate and even
His agent. Therefore, by propitiating Satan, whom
they percipiently represent by a peacock, they
venerate his superior; and why should they suffer
for it? On the other hand, if in the final outcome
of things the devil proves superior to God, they have
already taken the precaution of demonstrating
respect for that malevolent antideity, Satan.

But God, for them, exists in both their sacred
books, *The Book of Revelation* and *The Black*

Book, even if He is a somewhat contradictory concept (as is usually the case with respect to man's creation of a deity for mankind). One secret Yezidi prayer hailing God (but always leaving the possibility of power for his archenemy—the peacock Iblis, or Satan—who, like Milton's, is an angel who fell from grace) runs accordingly:

> O God, you are, I am not;
> You are the master of the law, I am a slave,
> You do not move and you are multiple,
> You are small and you are great,
> You have no voice and you are the word.
> You are suffering and you are balm.
> You are the judge of kings and of beggars.
> O God, you are the emperor who rules over thrones,
> You are the creator of oxen and fish.

Yezidi prayer

I know of no other contemporary religion so formally based on pure reason as Yezidi mysticism, which hedges its bets. But the instinct to conciliate evil, the better to ward off worse, has persisted in many areas into relatively modern times. Even today, grim sacrifices and vestigial ceremonies occur in parts of the world regarded as uncivilized. Wicked spirits are driven out by spells, pushed away by blowing, banned by artificial barriers.

In Slavonic Europe, belief in the vampire endured in remote villages at least until World War II. It was common knowledge that such creatures could be recognized by their ruddy skins. They had to be beheaded and their corpses staked into their graves to render them impotent. And what, one may ask, about the formally acknowledged rites of exorcism still occasionally practiced by such sophisticated religions as the Roman and Anglican churches?

In Paris, in the Catholic cardinal-archbishop's archdiocese, there is an office for the approved exorcist, who still follows the rites and prayers laid down in the seventeenth century *Rituale Romanum*. The Anglican (Episcopalian) Church pursues similar custom and recommends even today that every bishop "appoint a priest as diocesan exorcist, and that in each province centers of training should be established, if possible in collaboration with our Roman Catholic brethren." In addressing the devil ("O Satan, enemy of the Faith, enemy of the human race, who creates death and steals life . . . thou old serpent") a more laudable ecumenicity may prevail than is usual in addressing God.

One might, I suppose, relate such mystical dark creeds as wizardry, shamanism, and voodoo to this same fascination (sometimes founded on fear alone and sometimes abetted by logic) with all kinds of devil worship. Once, in 1971, as a momentarily lapsing atheist, I admit I was tempted to seek extraterritorial aid by praying for my grandson, Jonathan, who then lay desperately ill in distant England while I, forsaken by my wife who had flown to London, was pursuing my journalistic trade in East Africa.

That part of the world still provides trade for sorcerers and I considered seeking solace with one known for his efficacy and repute. However, my temptation faded; I remembered that some years earlier, in the Mozambique jungle, I paid two widely esteemed spell casters generous sums to put a hex on the cable desk of *The New York Times*. After accepting my money, each successively apologized that transoceanic hexing was beyond his ken.

Although my own creed, as I have redundantly stated, is the tragic, lonely creed of atheism, all my ancestors have been Jews. One forebear, a farmer who was burned out by Colonel Banastre Tarleton's Tory raiders during the American Revolution, settled afterward north of the small city of New York. His son was to be locally known as "Uncle Ben Hays, the only Jew and the best Christian in Westchester county."

Neither of my parents were true believers. I would say agnosticism rather than atheism would describe their theological approach. As a boy, reared in the countryside, I was occasionally sent to Sunday school, which I enjoyed immensely because the teacher's son had the finest collection of tin soldiers I had ever seen and we played with them after instruction in divinity. As a protest against war, my father had forbidden such deadly toys to me. Shortly thereafter both my parent and his brothers were to become officers in the U. S. Army.

Except when in Nazi Germany and, more recently, in Arab lands, I have never proclaimed myself a Jew when asked to provide data on the endless bureaucratic forms devoured by contemporary society; "atheist," after all, is the correct terminology in tolerant (if inquisitive) lands. However, I have told my children the only religious bequest I can make to them (since I decline to recommend my anticreed to anyone) is to call themselves Jews for reasons of pride so long as the term remains unpopular— which, alas, has been the case throughout most of recorded time.

In this analysis, or prelude, which cannot but be personal in approach and discursive in elaboration, I have mentioned much from Christian or Moslem orthodoxy to the demonological or Yezidi side of ritualism, which is less intricate. And I have discussed all this with no thought of levity. Religion, all religion, is a tender, precious thing for those who believe.

The divine side of ritual is infinitely more beautiful and more variegated than the satanic; also what we like to call more "civilized." I say "civilized" in quotation marks because, since the beginning of history, as many people have been cruelly killed in the name of one or another god as for any other reason. And intensely involved in this divine side is the widespread rite of prayer.

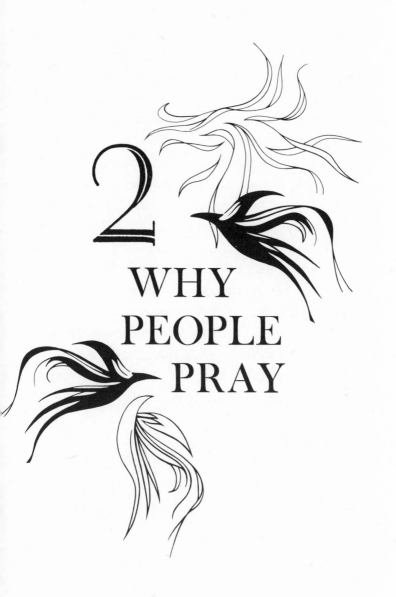

2

WHY PEOPLE PRAY

The noises of pain are often expressed in prayer and arise with daylight, which is to say consciousness of existence. There are various kinds of prayer; they derive from various impulses and they seek various results. But the habit is deeply rooted in humanity.

"If we traverse the world," Plutarch observed nineteen centuries ago, "it is possible to find cities without walls, without letters, without kings, without wealth, without coin, without schools and theatres; but a city without a temple, or that practiseth not worship, prayers and the like, no one ever saw."

This statement is still largely true—despite the spread of Marxism, whose expressions all share a common atheist factor. But the German's god-lessness has nothing to do with mine; it ardently proselytizes while I wish my gloom on no one else.

Communism, though materialist, has its own aspect of spirituality. It also has a methodology that in certain senses approximates religious forms. We might do well to remember that Buddhism, one of the world's great religions, does not advocate belief in God. Is it too shocking to consider communism another manifestation of that delightful human instinct, the desire to create in its own image something higher?

I don't know what could be classified as a Marxist equivalent of prayer, as it is known in other credos, even if the symbolism of a lithograph of Lenin still features what used to be called the icon corner in many a Russian dwelling. And the immense communist mausoleums—in Moscow, in Sofia, in Prague —combine the vainglorious religiosity of death in Pharaonic Egypt with baroque Christian Rome. There must be something in all this, some link, and whatever else let us not forget that pomp and yearning are human sentiments and prayer a wide-spread human habit.

"Pray without ceasing," counseled Saint Paul. "Praying is better than drinking, and much more pleasant to God," said the martyred Sir Thomas More.

Martin Luther advised:

> It is well to let prayer be the first employment in the early morning and the last in the evening. Avoid diligently those false and deceptive thoughts which say, "wait a little. I will pray an hour hence; I must first perform this or that." For with such thoughts a man quits prayer for business, which lays hold of and entangles him so that he comes not to pray the whole day long.

Dean Rusk, a former U. S. secretary of state, highly moral and upright although not himself a praying man, never forgot the words told him as a child by a circuit-riding preacher in the South: "Pray as if it were up to God; work as if it were up to you."

Swedenborg concluded: "Truth is what prays in man and a man is continually at prayer when he lives according to truth." Emily Dickinson, with delicate pathos, wrote: "Prayer is the little imple-ment through which men reach where presence is denied them." Ralph Waldo Emerson, touched with

New England practicality, assumed: "No man ever prayed heartily without learning something."

Seneca decided: "Fear drives the wretched to prayer." The New Testament Book of Matthew argued, like contemporary advertising: "All things, whatsoever ye shall ask in prayer, believing, ye shall receive." Islam's Koran includes in its daily quintuple rites of praying a form of healthy exercise, the physical reflection of devotion.

Chaucer suggested: "Whoso will pray, he must fast and be clean. And fat his soul, and make his body lean." Fénelon, with admirable French analysis, explained that, "He who desires not from the bottom of his heart, offers a deceitful prayer." Juvenal sensibly proposed: "You should pray for a sound mind in a sound body; for a stout heart that has no fear of death."

Pythagoras was enough of a scientist to be a skeptic, and cautioned: "Do not pray for yourself: you do not know what will help you." To which Seneca appended: "Don't ask for what you'll wish you hadn't got." Aeschylus warned, as if from experience: "God answers sharp and sudden on some prayers." Oscar Wilde sourly observed: "When the gods wish to punish us they answer our prayers." And Rabindranath Tagore admitted: "I quake in fear lest my prayer be granted."

There is a Scots proverb that says: "He has mickle prayer but little devotion." Lessing, the German poet, believed: "A single grateful thought toward heaven is the most complete prayer."

Juvenal recommended: "Leave it to the gods to decide what is best for us and most suitable to our circumstances." Menander restrained himself; he recalled: "Let not that happen which I wish, but that which is right." The lusty Rabelais wrote: "A short prayer enters heaven; a long drink empties the can." And Ovid ruefully put period to the argument: "Do not waste time in praying."

People are inclined to pray for everything and out of every motive: out of fear because they are terrified of dying or its consequence; to arouse combative spirit or martial confidence during war; out of despair; for mercy; in request of solace or of special favors; and sometimes out of sheer love, exuberance, or reverence.

Stalin insisted that the most powerful motivating force of human accomplishment was terror. De Gaulle believed it to be ambition or a sense of adventure. Probably both were right, for different kinds of men (De Gaulle's being the more pleasant).

Between these poles, disparate as they are in terms of mankind's character, one finds a broad range of prayers or pseudo-prayers, some confided to known or unknown gods and others to fellow men, either with the intent to comfort them (as was the case with Socrates) or to boast of the joys of life before departing it forever.

At either extreme the thought of terror, which guides so many a frightened soul, plays no role. Certainly the philosopher is rare who remains wholly uninfluenced by the Stalinist concept, yet the greatest among them was surely never a coward, even for a single flickering moment. In what is as true a prayer as any ever uttered, that brave Athenian said:

> I ought to be grieved at death, if I were not persuaded in the first place that I am going to other gods who are wise and good (of which I am certain as I can be of any such matters), and secondly (though I am not so sure of this last) to men departed, better than those whom I leave behind; and therefore I do not grieve as I might have done, for I have good hope that there is yet something remaining for the dead. . . .
>
> *Socrates*

Such comfort is derived from perusal of Plato's Socratic *Dialogues* that, even today, their tranquility and benign inspiration can serve as a substitute for more conventional types of prayer. I remember, years ago when entering hospital for a major operation whose outcome was in some doubt, that I wanted no one, not even my wife and children or my mother (then still alive) to know of it. Why worry people? While there is a chance, I reasoned, this is needless.

So, confiding my whereabouts only to one trusted friend that he might be able to find me (or my doctor) if worse came to worst, I took to my bed of pain a hired record player with selected works of Bach, Vivaldi, and Albenone, and my treasured Socrates, fully assured that thus I should be well entertained and spiritually enriched while awaiting my moment in time to end—if end it then must.

Another form of pseudo-prayer, in the Gaullist sense of ambition, was written in his diary by the last of the Serbian hajduks who was slain by Jugoslav gendarmes in 1938. *Hajduk* is an honorable term in southern Slav history and legend. It refers to a kind of Robin Hood phenomenon, men who for centuries fought the Ottoman Turkish occupiers of their lands, men who slew the tyrant, took from the rich (who were generally collaborators), and gave to the poor.

But the last hajduk, who died just before World War II, was merely a conventional brigand who lived by robbery and lust. Yet, vaunting the claim of hajduk, he received the help of peasants (whom he rewarded) in his own and their perpetual fight with that symbol of governing and tax collecting, the gendarme.

None was to come after him, only the succession of partisans and *četniks* who fought guerrilla wars against a later generation of occupying forces (and each other), in military units, not as individual folkloric bandits. And he, Pavle Dokić, was hunted to a lonely mountain heath by his uniformed enemies. There, surrounded by police forces hemming him ever closer in, Pavle raped a lovely young shepherd girl who stabbed him in the vitals with his own knife. He slew her and then, dying in an isolated bosk where he was later found, completed the last entry in his journal, boasting:

> In Heaven there is one God and one Pavle Dokić on earth. Only these two remain powerful. The world will remember the last hajduk. I will have a step like a

youth. And I will travel like a hero. And will feed
like a wolf. I will be like God in Heaven; for now
we remain, only us two, He in Heaven and I
on earth. As we hajduks say, so must it be;
and there will always be us hajduks. For the forest
without hajduks cannot be, as Heaven without God.
Here I have arrived this lovely summer to freedom
in the open spaces, to hear what I have most loved on
earth, that players play for me a parade march
and the Turkish rastanak and the Gjurdjevski kolo
and Tamo Daleko. Sadness for others I have lived
through. I have lived that the whole people know me.
On all sides is my portrait.

Pavle Đokić's Diary

Fear, I would imagine (with Seneca), is the most
commonplace inspirational force in this age of
unbelief; only the sudden approach of one of the four
apocalyptic horsemen is likely to stimulate recourse
by "the wretched" to a ritual abandoned by so
many out of laziness even if they may still profess
themselves believers. Indeed, I have doubted my own
atheism on occasion (as I earlier confessed) and
for an instant wondered if it was worth falling
back on the childlike habits of asking immediate
help of an unknown power. Fortunately I have
for the most part had enough self-control to avoid
such humiliation to a carefully nurtured if unpleasant
pride. But there is one prayer I would commend to
anyone suddenly staring over the precipice of death:

> Accustom yourself to thinking of death as nothing at all,
> since pleasure and pain exist only in sensation.
> It follows from this that a clear understanding of
> this fact that death is nothing allows us to enjoy this

mortal life and at the same time obviates our speculating on the life eternal, relieving us of the regret of immortality. Because there is nothing to be feared in the fact that we live just as there is nothing to fear in the fact that we do not live.

Epicurus

Once during World War II, I was aboard a military transport bound for England and, with busted instruments in a dense fog, we flew over German-occupied Holland, a fact recalled to us by the sudden arrival of a spitting Nazi night fighter zooming out of the dark. Seated beside a colonel who, with three aides, was bringing a half dozen new-type quick-opening parachutes over for testing, I broke the headset attached to a radio beside me so we each could listen in to one earpiece. "This is Great Joy Queen, Great Joy Quee-an," came the captain's somber voice. "Don't know where we are, don't know where we aaa-rrrr-e. Running out of fuel. Running out of fuu-elll."

Then, in from the crew compartment burst a sergeant radioman, burly, with steatopygous behind, sweating great drops although it was unmistakably cold. He said no word, simply strapped himself into one of several empty seats, clasped his hands together like a massive choirboy, clenched his eyes . . . and prayed. "Don't tell anybody what you've got in those parcels," I suggested to the colonel, nodding at the bulky packaged parachutes wrapped in burlap at the rear, "or you'll be mobbed."

I admit I have been frightened enough to think

of praying many a time, not being overendowed with what the French call *cran*. As a twenty-two-year-old reporter in Depression Pittsburgh, I was taken behind a garage by the strike-breaking thugs of two fink gangs led respectively by gentlemen called Whitey Williams and Eat-'Em-Up-Alive Jack McDade. Their announced intention was to give me a thrashing I would never forget because they had caught me taking down license numbers of cars transporting their strong-arm guards. Luckily, some unsuspected oratorical genius descended upon me and I was able to talk my way to a telephone—and my city editor—before they carried out their threat.

Locked up in Vienna's morgue by my own request (accompanied by bribes to the proper officials) just after Hitler's Anschluss, and inspecting the sheet-covered corpses of Jews who had been beaten or tortured to death, I became so appalled that until the keeper (whose palm had been well greased) opened the portal at dawn, I spent the whole night too astounded to be terrified . . . or even to think of prayer. And speedy frights—like landing in an Antarctic whiteout when you can't even see the hand you hold before you, or feeling your airplane crash into an Irish house—allow no time for submission to proper fear or instinctive prayer.

There are moments, I suspect, when any man—even those bolder and with greater souls than mine—may at one or another instant hearken to the voice of fear, even those endowed, as André Malraux said of De Gaulle, with "geological courage." At such a time the man with religious faith automatically seeks solace and strength from divinity. To those who, like myself, simply cannot in all honesty have recourse to others than himself, I recommend only these simple words:

> Prayer for a brave heart, which does not fear death,
> Which places a long life last among the gifts
> Of nature, which has the power to endure any trials,
> Rejects anger, discards desire.

Juvenal

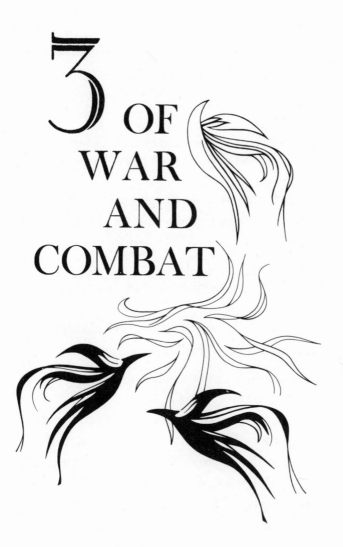

3 OF
WAR
AND
COMBAT

It is noteworthy that military men, who know death at least as well as priests, are, as a profession, almost as given to praying.

It takes a courageous man to face his end, above all if it be painful, without prior preparation in the form of prayer. Few are so wise as Epictetus, who resigned himself with sad good sense:

> Do with me as thou wilt; my will is thy will;
> I appeal not against thy judgments.

These are the words of the philosopher, not the warrior who, with that splendid English king, Alfred, would urge:

> If thou hast a woe, tell it not to the weakling.
> Tell it to thy saddle-bow and ride singing forth.

A more pragmatic and modest American chaplain proposed in World War II:

> Praise the Lord and pass the ammunition.

Of course, the most terrible and brutal conquerors were given to terrible and brutal prayers, if they reflected at all in a philosophical sense. The greatest Mongol who, when dying, bade the courtiers in his round, felt yurt: "Do not make a lament," once described with the relish of a successful warrior his "greatest joy." This was a form of shamanistic prayer:

> The greatest joy a man can know is to conquer his
> enemies and drive them before him. To ride
> their horses and take away their possessions.
> To see the faces of those who were dear to them

bedewed in tears, and to clasp their wives and daughters in his arms.

Genghis Khan

This bitter paean reminds me of the nineteenth-century Spanish dictator, shriven on his deathbed, who sat bolt upright when asked to forgive his enemies. "Father," he told the priest, "I have none. I have had them all killed."

Most professional men of war become wholly obsessed with their search for victory and are oblivious to fear or, indeed, other sensations. That lovely Welsh compilation, *The Mabinogion,* tells us of the knight Peredur who fought on the blood-spattered snow and, while he did not truly pray in the usual sense of that word, simply reflected on the beauty of his lady. These meditations in a strange way became the loveliest if most formless of prayers.

> "And Peredur stood, and compared the blackness of the raven, and the whiteness of the snow, and the redness of the blood, to the hair of the lady whom best he loved, which was blacker than it, and to her skin which was whiter than snow, and to the two red spots upon her cheeks, which were redder than the blood upon the snow appeared to be." As he muses thus he is accosted by twenty-four knights in succession, and so deep is his meditation that he cannot answer them, but when they attack him he throws each in turn to the ground with one thrust of his lance, and finally overthrows his enemy, Sir Kai, and rides over him twenty-one times without disturbing the train of his meditation.

Mabinogion

We are told of another legendary hero by the musical Welsh, whose Celtic memory seems as ancient as the seams of coal that line their poor green valleys:

> It is said of Conchubar that he had been
> desperately wounded in the head, and was told that,
> in order to save his life, he must keep quiet and
> refrain from anger. This he did for seven years,
> but on one Friday he beheld the sun and moon
> darkened at mid-day, and was told that at this very hour
> Jesus Christ was being crucified. Forthwith the old
> pagan king burst into a terrible cry of grief and rage.
>   Forthwith he rushed out with his sword,
> and began hacking the branches of an oakwood,
> since there were no Jews at hand on whom his
> vengeance might be wreaked. And in so doing
> he opened the old wound in his head, and fell lifeless
> among the trees.
>
> *Conchubar of Wales*

Between the poetic repose of Peredur and the savage madness of Conchubar we see the extent to which men differ in thoughts or in their lack when approaching combat, and how violence can expose strange inner qualities in humans. I have plied the trade of war correspondent as a kind of jackal with a typewriter, accompanying some dozen formal or informal armies at various times of this sick and melancholy century. And I have often and again been struck by the self-confidence of that tough, brave, fair-play confraternity who, like La Hire, Joan of Arc's doughty captain, ask only an even break of God:

Sire Dieu, I pray to you to do for La Hire
What La Hire would do for You
Were you captain-at-arms and he God.

I have no idea what La Hire looked like, but somehow am convinced he must have resembled that
later warrior, Anne de Montmorency, constable of
France, whose massive suit of armor, fit for an
immense gorilla, features the collection in New
York's Metropolitan Museum.

It has always seemed to me that La Hire, as he
emerges down the corridor of history, confirms that
the brave and hardy Maid of Orleans was more
devout peasant than mystic saint. For her principal
commander would surely have sworn allegiance
more easily to a tough soldier-patriot, even if un-
taught in current strategies of war, than to a
delicate, nunlike flower.

However, there may be more to this than can
ever be known. André Malraux astutely points out
that Isabeau de Bavière, mother of King Charles
VII, was famed for her wanton affairs and fruit-
fulness. Malraux gives credence to the tale that Joan
(or Jeannette, as she was called in her native village)
was in fact half sister of the sovereign whose throne
her military exploits won back for him.

La Hire (whose real name was Etienne de
Vignoles) seems by the very wording of his prayers
to be of the true orthodox tradition of bluff commanders. His man-to-man relationship with
divinity was surely paralleled by that fine royalist

leader in England's seventeenth-century civil war, Major General Sir Jacob Astley. Just before the Battle of Edgehill began (1642), Astley addressed himself on high and said:

> Lord, I shall be verie busie this day: I may forget Thee, but doe Thou not forget me!

He then looked around him and added "March on, boys." Astley was captured four years later at Stow-on-the-Wold. A philosophical man, he told his captors: "You have now done your work and may goe and play, unless you will fall out amongst yourselves."

The sporting military prayer addressed to God in hopes of an even break may be aptly classified as the "Don't-help-that-bear" plea, after Daniel Boone's special request of the Supreme Being:

> Lord. If You can't help me, don't help that bear.

It is an exceedingly familiar form of prayer to followers of the martial trade. They are, after all, used to enduring the hard knocks of war, and they are also more reconciled than most to that possibility of bad luck which only heavenly favor can keep from rendering catastrophic.

Daniel, Earl of Nottingham, who commanded the forces of King William of Orange once the latter had taken over England, sent his troops off with this Protestant admonition against the Catholic French:

> In Thy name, oh God, do we set up our banners. Go forth, therefore, with our fleets and armies, that through

> Thee we may do valiantly. And do Thou, oh Lord of Hosts, tread down our enemies. Plead our cause against an ungodly nation.

I have never ceased to marvel at the presumption of so many believers that God himself favors their own particular sect, their special interpretation of His alleged prejudices or intentions, or at least that He frowns upon their opponents. This of course has led to the unpleasant fact that to date, as I have already mentioned, more men have killed each other in the name of God than for any other single cause—if cause it be. For after all, both sides usually importune divine assistance and one side loses in the end.

Yet the illogic of supposing God's sectarianism has long been supposed also to have strategic value. Field Marshal, Prince Leopold I of Anhalt-Dessau, a burning Lutheran and brilliant Prussian general, at the field of Kesselsdorf (1745) asked only this of Heaven:

> Oh Lord God, let me not be disgraced in my old days. Or if Thou wilt not help me, do not help these scoundrels; but leave us to try it ourselves.

Then he proceeded to overwhelm the Catholic forces of Austria lined up before his guns.

Among the ancient Jews—a belligerent and durable people—Flavius Josephus (himself a former Jewish general who turned collaborator and worked for the Romans) tells us of two heroes who fought in God's name, one successfully, one in glorious disaster. The first, who led a searing revolt against the might of Rome, addressed his troops accordingly, says Josephus in his remarkable history:

> O my fellow-soldiers, no other time remains more opportune than the present for courage and contempt of dangers; for if you now fight manfully, you may recover your liberty, which as it is a thing of itself agreeable to all men, so it proves to be to us much more desirable, by its affording us the liberty of worshipping God.

Judas Maccabaeus

But the result of the famous Maccabean insurrec-rection came later. After some generations a legion conquered Jerusalem and another besieged the craggy, barren fortress of Masada, above the Dead Sea, where Eleazar, chief of the fanatical patriotic sect of Zealots, held out until his stronghold's walls were battered down by Roman artillery. Then when collapse, defeat, murder, rapine, and slavery had become inevitable, he summoned the survivors and urged them, again in the name of God:

> Let our wives die before they are abused, and our children before they have tasted of slavery; and after we have slain them, let us bestow that glorious benefit upon one another mutually, and preserve ourselves in freedom, as an excellent funeral monument for us. But first let us destroy our money and the fortress by fire; for I am well assured that this would be a grief to the Romans, that they shall not be able to seize upon our bodies, and shall fail of our wealth also: and let us spare nothing but our provisions; for they will be a testimonial when we are dead that we were not

subdued for want of necessaries, but that, according to our original resolution, we have preferred death before slavery.

Next day, the legionnaires clambered across wreckage occasioned by their battering rams and catapults, and entered Masada. They were astounded to find piles of bodies—some killed in battle, others obviously slaughtered by each other, but all dead.

Another victim of Rome's incredible military might was Hannibal, the brilliant Carthaginian whose infantry, bowmen, and elephants had almost brought the mighty empire down. His prayer was simple and final, as Polybius tells us in his account of the Punic Wars:

> Hannibal, when surrounded, called for poison, long kept in readiness, and said: "Let us release the Romans from their anxiety, since they think it too long to wait for the death of an old man."

But the poor Roman soldiers themselves, who fought all over the known world on behalf of their gods and their efficient society, were also deserted over and over again in their lonely outposts of glory. We are reminded of this in the following sad plea, found recently on the edge of the Saharan waste:

> Make haste to reassure me, I beg of you, and tell me that our fellow-citizens understand us, support us and protect us as we ourselves are protecting the glory of the Empire.
> If it should be otherwise, if we should have to leave

our bleached bones on these desert sands in vain,
then beware of the anger of the Legions!

Marcus Flavinius, Centurion on the
Second Cohort of the Augusta Legion

Gore is the customary coinage of conquest, and
in olden days divinity was beseeched to provide
ambitious armies with talented carnage-spilling
leadership. Thus we have this ghastly if traditional
type of prayer from a Persian overlord:

> Lord of the seven planets, send us a blood-thirsty king
> so that Dardasht's plain may be leveled, and Jubareh
> streams flow with blood.
> Add to the numbers of our people, so that each one
> may be rent into two hundred pieces.

Kamal-uddin Ismail of Isfahan

More primitive peoples tended not to call on the
gods for help, but to incorporate their magical
powers in their own human heroes, as for example
the Tsimshian group of tribes that dotted the
coastline of the Northwest Pacific. One of their
texts recounts:

> An arrow struck the eye of one of the brothers
> [children of Hîslēgiyōôntk, chief in heaven].
> Their sister sucked it out, and the wound closed again.
> After some time the eldest brother shouted,
> "Stop fighting, else I shall turn over my club,
> and your town will be buried. Trees will grow up
> in its place." When they continued the fight,
> he turned his club, and the whole town disappeared
> under ground. Trees grew in its place. Then he

turned his club again and the town reappeared,
but the G·itg·initō'x continued to fight.

*The Origin of the G-ispawaduwe'da
(told by Chief Mountain)*

But as death became more mechanized in modern
days, a relative moderation crept into the requests of
army commanders. They still pleaded—if anything
more fervently—for heavenly intercession on their behalf,
but they toned down the degree of ferocity requested.
Oddly enough, there is something more modest
then the ringing challenges of La Hire and Anhalt-
Dessau in the prayer of the usually conceited victor
of the Battle of El Alamein on the eve of that
decisive victory in 1942:

> Therefore let every officer and man enter the battle
> with a stout heart, and the determination to
> do his duty so long as he has breath in his body.
> *And let no man surrender so long as he is unwounded
> and can fight.*
> Let us all pray that "the Lord mighty in battle"
> will give us the victory.

*Lieutenant General Bernard Law (later
Field Marshal Lord) Montgomery*

It is not surprising that less than two years later,
on the eve of the Normandy landings which broke the
back of Hitler's "Fortress Europe," the Supreme
Allied Commander, always a far more humble
man than his brash British subordinate, should
have addressed his troops accordingly:

> You are about to enter upon the great crusade
> toward which we have striven these many months. . . .

Good luck. And let all beseech the blessing of
Almighty God upon this great and noble undertaking.

General Dwight D. Eisenhower

I am struck by the large proportion of naval
commanders who seem to emerge, when confronting
death and the Lord of all battles, as more diffident
than their peers on land vis-à-vis divinity, even
though equally resolute when facing the imminence
of danger. Is there something about the clean sea
winds that blows away the tarnish of human arro-
gance from such bold brows as that of Nelson?
Of this group of seamen, I would cite the little-
known British officer who composed a prayer in
1941 for his ship, a prayer called to my attention
by George Seferis, the Greek Nobel Prize poet:

> O God our loving Father . . . Help us to keep in mind
> the real causes of war: dishonesty, greed, selfishness,
> and lack of love, and to drive them out of this ship,
> so that she may be a pattern of the new world
> for which we are fighting. . . .

Lord Hugh Beresford, Royal Navy

There is the eminently practical, commonsensical
approach (already mentioned earlier) of that tough
U. S. Navy chaplain fighting back at Japanese planes
in the most disastrous surprise attack of World War II.

Praise the Lord and pass the ammunition.

*Howell Maurice Forgy (on board the
cruiser New Orleans, Pearl Harbor,
December 7, 1941)*

And finally the shipboard services at the Newfoundland meeting of those indomitable giants of the war, Churchill and Roosevelt, when they conspired and planned as if the neutral United States were already a belligerent. Perhaps it was the briny, summer, offshore breeze that inspired such a humble, pitying mood:

> We bring before Thee, O Lord, the griefs and perils of people and nations; the sighing of prisoners; the necessities of the homeless; the helplessness of the weak; the pains of the sick and wounded; the sorrows of the bereaved. Comfort and relieve them, O Merciful Father, according to their several needs, for the sake of Thy Son, our Saviour and Christ. AMEN.
>
> *From the Prayers Used at the Church Service Sunday Morning, 10 August 1941, on the Quarter-Deck of H. M. S.* Prince of Wales, *at Sea, and Attended by Franklin D. Roosevelt, President of the United States, and the Prime Minister of Great Britain, Winston S. Churchill*

Strangely, for so ungentle and cocky a man, this same modest spirit of reverence can be detected in the words of Queen Elizabeth's boldest admiral, regarded by the Spaniards as a brutal pirate, that eventual victor over King Philip's great Armada:

> O Lord God, when Thou givest to Thy servants to endeavor any great matter, grant us also to know that it is not the beginning, but the continuing of the game until it be thoroughly finished, which yieldeth the true glory; through Him that for the finishing of Thy work laid down His life, our Redeemer, Jesus Christ. Amen.
>
> *Sir Francis Drake (sailing in to raid Cadiz, 1587)*

Perhaps the noblest of all these gun-inspired prayers was that signaled by England's greatest seaman of all time; though audacious and highly braggart himself, he caught the spirit of superhuman obligation at a turning point in history (which slew him):

> May the Great God, whom I worship, grant to my country and for the benefit of Europe in general, a great and glorious victory, and may no misconduct in anyone tarnish it; and may humanity after victory be the predominant feature in the British fleet!
>
> *Horatio, Lord Nelson (before the Battle of Trafalgar, 1803)*

So, finally, the road from war takes us back to one more general, this century's least humble man, who, on the occasion of receiving the surrender of Imperial Japan, yet bowed down to his God with simplicity—perhaps because he stood on the deck of a battleship and not amid the smoking debris of a battlefield (there is something somehow cleaner about ships):

> Let us pray that peace be now restored to the world, and that God will preserve it always.
> These proceedings are closed.
>
> *General Douglas MacArthur (after the surrender of the Japanese aboard the battleship* Missouri, *September 2, 1945)*

4 OF AWE, LOVE & EXUBERANCE

I am fascinated by prayers because so frequently they tend to reveal the secret reaction of humans subjected to exceptional stress, and also they expose the weaknesses which, to one or another degree, exist in all of us. The most philosophical of those anthologized in these pages are represented by Sir Thomas More's exhortation of brotherhood:

> We be glad to think it well done to
> pray every poor man to pray for us.

Some men get the God they deserve and some the devil they desire, which is really not surprising since unknown eons ago mankind chose to create God (or the devil) in his own image. At first— before dim apprehensions of initial logic told humans that something existed before them or their universe and would therefore exist after them and their universe (a quite unprovable assumption)— gods and devils were inanimate objects: rocks, trees, fire, water, the sun, the moon.

It was to be many centuries before man endowed these frightening conceptions with a form resembling his own, if usually on a grander scale. However, it is to be noted (as I have said), most of the earliest such divinities were female, like Inana, Astarte, Ishtar, and Gaia, the earth mother. It was comparatively late in human life that men were recognized as playing any role in procreation of the species. Only after this discovery, and after men grew relatively larger than their mates, when they roved afield on muscular hunts while mothers with their babies led a sedentary life, did male gods—and male devils—gain ascendency.

The change in symbolized divinity—first from inanimate to animate, then, by sex, from female to to male—was never quite successfully achieved with regard to immortality. As Sir James George Frazer noted in *The Golden Bough,* since man made his deities in his own likeness and was himself mortal, he naturally supposed his divine creations to be in the same sad predicament. Frazer cited Greenland Eskimos as convinced their god would die if he touched a dog. He recalled the distantly separated cases of the dead god Dionysus, whose grave was at Delphi; the grave of Zeus in Crete; and the grave of a Filipino tribal Creator atop Mount Cabunian—all as mortal as those poor earthlings who worshiped them.

More complicated and intellectual religions have sought in different ways to bridge the conceptual gap between human mortality, which invented God, and divine immortality, the principal impulse for that invention. Christianity resolves the paradox by the slaying and resurrection of a man who was likewise God's son and God himself. Islam teaches terrestrial-style immortality transported to Heaven (allowing for the Prophet's own millennial return to earth). And Hinduism explains successive, endless cycles of reincarnation.

Once male domination had been accepted as a sexual fact, after centuries of mother adoration, it was taken for granted in all relatively modern faiths that God or the principal god was a man. Religion is in need of its women's lib today.

The question of God's color was never discussed. Since human attributes were ascribed to Him, His pigmentation was the same as that of the dominant race wherever He was revered, from India to Palestine; and also, I might add, for several decades in Africa and South America, where His skin was held to be as white as those of the martial priests who had imposed Him. His features in the Orient were marked by the Mongol fold; in the Occident by Caucasian angularity.

As for God's language, clearly a requisite for effective praying, the Emperor Charles V recommended that Spanish was obviously desirable. Jewish scholars, however, were positive that either Hebrew or Aramaic was the theological tongue for converse with divinity, never agreeing on which. The school of Rabbi Johanan favored the former and Rabbi Judah the latter.

The Armenians held that theirs was the language spoken by God to Noah, but medieval theologians proved to their own satisfaction that Eve was seduced in Italian, Adam misled in Czech, both were scolded in German by the Lord, and were expelled from Eden in Hungarian by the Archangel Gabriel. The Shiite Persians, by the way, claimed that Gabriel spoke Turkish, most menacing of tongues. This linguistic question is, in theory, vital. If the true believer is to pray to his deity he must find a means of accurately expressing his desires, if not his thoughts.

As I have said, I am personally an atheist and expect to live and die in that lonely state. For me atheism simply renounces the artificial logic on which the poetry of religion is based. I do not believe in God. I do believe in accident or what some may call nature. Why should life have a motive? Or a beginning? Or an end?

However, while thus removing myself from the doctrines founded on what we call faith—a very indifferent substitute for reason—I am nevertheless, being human, not free of all respect for ritual; nor do I wish to be, as ritual can be a lovely experience. In this I find my reactions somewhere between those of Jean-Paul Sartre and Ezra Pound. The former wrote:

> Even if I think it is God that I obey, it is I who decided that it was God who spoke to me.
>
> *Jean-Paul Sartre*

And the latter, that half-mad American genius:

> O bright Apollo,
> Τίν᾽ ἄνδρα, τὶν᾽ ἥρωα, τίνα θεὸν,
> What god, man, or hero,
> Shall I place a tin wreath upon!
>
> *Ezra Pound*

While generally a prayer is regarded as a plea for help or consolation to someone in authority, most often God Himself, certain prayers ask nothing, but merely express sheer exuberance or joy. Hermann Hesse confides:

> I just love the stone and the river and all these things
> that we see and from which we can learn. I can love
> a stone, Govinda, and a tree or a piece of bark. These
> are things and one can love things. But one cannot
> love words. Therefore teachings are of no use to me;
> they have no hardness, no softness, no colors, no corners,
> no smell, no taste—they have nothing but words.
>
> *Hermann Hesse*

This is the same joyous acceptance expressed by the ancient Egyptians to their eternally generous sun:

> Beautiful is thine appearing in the horizon of heaven,
> thou living sun, the first who lived! Thou risest in the
> eastern horizon, and fillest every land with thy beauty.
> . . . The birds fly out of their nests and their wings
> praise thy ka. All wild beasts that dance on their feet, all
> that fly and flutter—they live when thou arisest for them.
> . . . The fishes leap up before thy face. Thy rays are
> in the sea.
>
> *Book of the Dead*

These remarkable, poetic inhabitants of the world's oldest nation-state (older even than venerable China) also wrote with gratitude of their first monotheistic divinity:

> He [Amun] who made the herbage [for] the cattle,
> And the fruit tree for mankind,
> Who made that [on which] the fish of the river
>   may live,
> And the birds soaring in the sky.
> He who gives breath to that which is in the egg,
> Gives life to the son of the slug,
> And makes that on which the gnats may live,

And worms and flies in like manner;
Who supplies the needs of the mice in their holes
And gives life to flying things in every tree.
Hail to Thee, who did all this!

Egyptian "Hymn to Amun-Re"

The roster of saints (as duly accredited by the hierarchies of their respective faiths) is replete with names of those good, grateful, and usually pious souls who thanked the heavens above for providing so many beautiful experiences for little man to enjoy during his brief moment aboard humanity's ark.

On the canonical list of Rome, apart from St. John of the Cross, this heathen's favorite is Francis of Assisi; I am especially pleased that at the little Tuscan hill-town of his birth (where Francis, as a young man, spent some years as local rake and cutup) one of the loveliest churches in all Christendom still honors his gentle soul. This church is as pure and clean, fine and multihued as was that thirteenth-century embodiment of human kindness.

Francis clearly considered himself the blood relative of all that was fair, charming, and graceful, from the wind and the water to the birds and the beasts. He has always seemed to me a kind of poetic pantheist, a Christian Jain, widely removed from the doctrinal discipline of Rome. He prayed:

Praised be my Lord God for all his creatures, and especially for our brother the sun, who brings us the day and who brings us the light; fair is he and shines with a very great splendor: O Lord, he signifies to us thee!

Praised be my Lord for our sister the moon, and
for the stars, the which he has set clear and lovely
in heaven.

Praised be my Lord for our brother the wind, and
for air and cloud, calms and all weather, by which
thou upholdest life in all creatures.

Praised be my Lord for our sister water, who is
very serviceable unto us and humble and precious
and clean.

Praised be my Lord for our brother fire, through
whom thou givest us light in the darkness; and he
is bright and pleasant and very mighty and strong.

Praised be my Lord for our mother the earth, the
which doth sustain us and keep us and bringeth
forth divers fruits and flowers of many colors,
and grass.

St. Francis of Assisi

Gazing from the gay frescoes of Giotto in the
saint's memorial church to the rolling, wind-stroked
hills of Tuscany, one can still hear the fragile
whisper of his words caressing the memory he left
behind.

And that other elegant spirit, Saint John? Juan
de Yepez y Alvarez (who later adopted the name
Juan de la Cruz) was a sixteenth-century Castilian
mystic broken by persecution during Spain's harsh
Counter-Reformation period. He died in a stern
monastery and was only admitted by bureaucratic
Rome into the sainthood of dogmatic recognition a
century and a half later. Yet the rapturous poems
he composed amid his sorrows are among the most
profoundly moving and ecstatic of anything written

in any of man's many languages. Hearken to these
words:

> O, guiding night;
> O, night more lovely than the dawn;
> O, night that hast united
> The lover with His beloved,
> And changed her into love . . .
>
> As I scattered His hair in the breeze
> Cuando yo sus cabellos esparcía.
>
> *St. John of the Cross*

It is truly—even more than with Homer or with
Virgil—impossible to seize the passion of Juan except
in his own exquisite version of the rich Spanish language:

> Míos son los cielos, y mía es la tierra,
> mías son las gentes, los justos son míos, y míos los
> pecadores, los angeles son míos, y la madre de dios
> y todas las cosas son mías, y el mismo dios es mío y
> para mí, porque XPO es mío y todo para mí;
> pues que pides y buscas alma mía tuyo es todo esto
> y todo es para ti.
>
> *St. John of the Cross*

Of other Catholic saints, many indeed are endowed
with modesty and aesthetic appreciation as well as
proper reverence for God. One can, on occasion,
even detect the outlines of a sense of humor—as
one sometimes startlingly observes, with that other
passionate Spaniard, St. Teresa of Avila.

Apart from her fierce devotion, she was among
the great organizers of eternal women's lib. She
was a kind of precursor of the efficient woman, subse-

quently so often to be gently mocked by male colleagues endowed with a superiority complex, or by apologetic females like the *New Yorker*'s Helen Hokinson.

Teresa, whose visions ranged from Heaven to hell, whose organizing efficiency was remarkable, who was shrewd and brave but also (one suspects) somewhat of a masochist, beat her contemporary, Juan de la Cruz, to official sainthood by a century. Her corpse was said to exude a violet odor, and one of its hands, cut off by an admirer, was found to work miracles. Nevertheless, mixed with all these astonishing qualities, she possessed a modest twinkle. Witness her brief prayer:

> May He be forever blessed,
> Who has endured me for so long. Amen.
>
> *St. Teresa of Avila*

Perhaps the most intellectual on Rome's holy list was Thomas of Aquino, a thirteenth-century Neapolitan nobleman with royal blood in his veins. He soon became reputed for his piety, his scholastic eminence, and for his extraordinary ability to synthesize—wedding, as it were, Aristotle to the most orthodox interpretations of Christian doctrine. That special genius led to the immortalizing of his own name in the Thomist dogmatic code.

Yet a slow, strong, heavy-set man with profound and orderly mind, he could cheerfully and gracefully acknowledge a modest role of human existence with respect to a cosmic pattern of beauty. That he

lacked the poetic felicity of a Francis or a John
of the Cross, when it came to expressing this appreciation, does not obscure its value:

> It is a great thing, a very great thing to be able to
> do without all solace, both human and divine,
> and to be willing to bear this exile of the heart (for
> the honor of God), and in nothing seek self, and not
> to have regard to one's own merit. What great thing
> is it to be cheerful and devout when grace comes to
> thee? This is an hour desirable to all.
>
> *St. Thomas Aquinas*

Acceptance, hope, happiness, and love mix with
awe and exuberance to comprise their own special
chapter in any anthology of prayer: a chapter of
appreciation rather than request for aid or solace.
And many are those of many differing faiths
(including even all lack of them) who contribute
to this cheerful list. As a fitful American genius
wrote:

> Ezra Pound, Augustus John
> Bless the bed that I lie on.
>
> *Ezra Pound*

Hope is perhaps the oldest contributing force to
human vigor or even to human resignation. The
eminently practical sixteenth-century Protestant
reformer, whose doctrine first officially acknowledged
the rights of the wealthy to qualify for Heaven, expressed this permanent dependence on hope accordingly:

> Tant que je respire, j'éspère.
>
> *John Calvin*

Likewise, happiness (which may be varyingly defined according to time, place, and the persons involved) is a common and understandable craving of mankind. Even the Buddhists, who venerate no formal monotheistic deity, share both the aspirations and methods of Occidental religions in this respect. Witness the following:

> May every living thing, movable or unmovable,
> tall, big, or medium-sized, clumsy or refined,
> visible or invisible, near or far, already born or
> aspiring to birth—may all beings have a happy heart.
>
> *Buddhist prayer*

Gerard Manley Hopkins, a nineteenth-century English Jesuit priest, was one of the most individual poets of his time, with a true perception of what beauty actually represented and what its specific components were. Hopkins, in terms of his own faith, was disregarded by never achieving recognition for taking even the first steps toward formal sainthood. This is a pity, for no one could have written his astonishing stanzas without having contained within his soul the necessary qualifications for that mark of religious esteem.

He was so restrained in his own delicacy, when viewing the possible implied contradictions between pure poetry and pure saintliness, that on entering the Society of Jesus he even burned his own youthful verses, which could not conceivably have contained anything less than lovely. What religious paean (save by Juan de la Cruz) could contain a

better marriage between godliness and loveliness
than Hopkins's:

> Glory be to God for dappled things—
> For skies of couple-color as a brindled cow;
> For rose-moles all in stipple upon trout that swim;
> Fresh-firecoal chestnut-falls; finches' wings;
> Landscape plotted and pieced—fold, fallow, and
>   plough;
> And all trades, their gear and tackle and trim.

Gerard Manley Hopkins

The gateway to happiness—or even its paradoxical,
often unhappy, form of ecstasy—is love. This is
acknowledged by clerical and lay authors throughout time, and love can be seen in differing forms, all
of them sharing the quality of radiance. Thus, from
the isles of classic Greece, a pantheistic love of beauty:

> Evening, thou that bringest all, whatever the light-
> giving dawn scattered; thou bringest the sheep, thou
> bringest the goat, thou bringest the child to its mother.

Sappho of Lesbos

Sappho was no saint, nor was Federico García
Lorca of the southern Spanish province of Granada,
a magnificent poet who was slaughtered by Fascists
in 1936 for the sin of being too left-wing for the taste
of General Franco's military insurrectionists. But
Lorca knew beauty (as even the political kin of his
murderers now admit). He wrote in *Bodas de Sangre:*

> Beautiful horseman,
> Now a heap of snow:
> He stormed hills and fairs
> And women's arms.   *García Lorca*

Pound, who keeps creeping into these primarily priestly pages, also knew beauty:

> When new love plucks the falcon from his wrist,
> And cuts the gyve and casts the scarlet hood,
> Where is the heron heart whom flight avails? . . .
> Lo! With a hawk of light thy love hath caught me.

Ezra Pound

And Shams al-Din Hafiz of Shiraz, in the ancient Persian province of Fars, a fourteenth-century mystic, could worship both the pleasure and pain of love:

> Love seemed at first an easy thing—
> But ah! the hard awakening . . .
> Within life's caravanserai
> What brief security have I,
> When momently the bell doth cry,
> "Bind on your loads; the hour is nigh!"

Hafiz

It is extraordinary how ubiquitous love is in the thoughts of men, and ascribed by all civilizations to an immensely variegated series of relationships—physical, spiritual, intellectual, mystical. Even the Peruvian Incas, renowned for the ferocity of their customs, above all with respect to religious worship, saw the reality of love and how it transcended mankind alone. In this case, it is with respect to their chief god, the all-powerful and glorious Viracocha:

> Oh conquering Viracocha!
> Ever-present Viracocha!
> Thou who art without equal upon the earth!

Thou who art from the beginnings of the world
    until its end.
Thou gavest life and valor to me, saying,
"Let this be a man."
And to woman, saying,
"Let this be a woman."
Thou madest them and gavest them being.
Watch over them, that they may live in health
    and in peace.
Thou who art in the highest heavens,
And among the clouds of the tempest,
Grant them long life,
And accept this our sacrifice,
Oh, Creator.

*Inca prayer (translated by Father
Molina of Cuzco)*

A heartbreaking plea for love was found on the
gold pendant of a girl buried at Aquincum (nowadays
called Budapest), the old Roman capital of Lower
Pannonia. On her treasured jewel, in Greek words,
this early Danubian beauty had caused to be wrtten:

Let them talk as much as they like.
I do not care.
Do love me: it will serve you well.

The greatest of all Russian writers saw love in its deep
truth against the full panoply of existence and, in
a strange way, consequently gave to this emotion its
most intensely religious description:

Love all God's creation, both the whole and
every grain of sand. Love every leaf, every ray of light.
Love the animals, love the plants, love each
separate thing. If thou love each thing thou wilt
perceive the mystery of God in all; and when

once thou perceive this, thou wilt thenceforward
grow every day to a fuller understanding of it:
until thou come at last to love the whole world
with a love that will then be all-embracing and universal.

Feodor Dostoevski

What one might call a more reposeful, tranquil
version of the same thought translated into Oriental
philosophy is ascribed to Yogi Milarepa, a medieval
Buddhist monk. Milarepa dwelt on the soaring
Himalayan slopes between Tibet and Nepal, leading
a solitary life of peaceful contemplation. He counseled:

May every one e'er practice the Sacred Dharma;
It bringeth Peace and Happiness to all.

Yogi Milarepa

Love in its philosophical meaning, as a code of
behavior and a way of life, was suggested by
Eusebius, Bishop of Caesarea, during the early
bloody days of Christianity when that new doctrine
was so often at war within its own disputatious
self. His offering was pure, but rarely put to practice
in Caesarea's quarrelsome see (even until today):

May I be no man's enemy, and may I be the friend
of that which is eternal and abides. May I never
quarrel with those nearest me; and if I do,
may I be reconciled quickly. May I never devise evil
against any man; if any devise evil against me,
may I escape uninjured and without the need of
hurting him. May I love, seek, and attain
only that which is good.

Eusebius, Bishop of Caesarea

In the end, most systems of religion or philosophy have counseled such search for goodness, love, and reconciliation for, after all, as the Sumerians learned so many centuries ago:

> In my city man dies, oppressed is the heart,
> Man perishes, heavy is the heart,
> I peered over the wall,
> Saw the dead bodies floating in the river's
>   waters,
> As for me, I too will be served thus, verily it is so!
> Man, the tallest, cannot reach to heaven,
> Man, the wildest, cannot cover the earth.
>
> *Gilgamesh*

Finally, to conclude these prayers of and pleas for love, a dreadful reminder from a little Jewish girl who knew very little of it from a harsh and brutal world. May one never forget that she, before she was taken away to butchers in a Nazi concentration camp, had confided to her secret diary words of the utmost wisdom, words of which any adult saint, poet, or philosopher could be proud:

> The best remedy for those who are afraid, lonely, or unhappy is to go outside, somewhere where they can be quite alone with the heavens, nature, and God. Because only then does one feel that all is as it should be and that God wishes to see people happy, amidst the simple beauty of nature. As long as this exists, and it certainly always will, I know that then there will always be comfort for every sorrow, whatever the circumstances may be.
>
> *Anne Frank*

5
FOR
SOLACE
OR SPECIAL
FAVORS

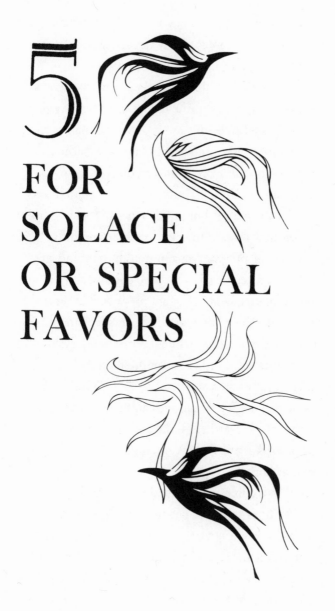

Most prayers, in most times and in most places, lack the concept of self-reliance demonstrated, for example, by La Hire. They tend to be more humble, more doubting, more wholly dependent, and (one might say) more implicitly skeptical.

Their conventional formulation is more often as an entreaty, frequently in the nature of actual begging, and addressed to beings more powerful than even the mightiest of mortal men. One early Latin definition of the word "prayer" derives from a modest approach to divinity, a petition, sometimes larded with praise; but another definition is simply: "An earnest request to someone for something."

The act of praying, so common to mankind in all ages and regions, is addressed most usually to God no matter what theology prevails. The similarity of the gods beseeched is less evident than that of the method by which they are addressed. Harry Emerson Fosdick, a commonsensical American preacher, warned his flock: "God is not a cosmic bellboy for whom we can press a button to get things." Nevertheless, the fact that this warning was needed confirms how often humanity entertains just that hope.

Man in trouble regards God as the great fixer, whether he is seen as a geometrician (Plato, Sir Thomas Browne), a carpenter (Erasmus), a refuge (Psalms), a fortress (Luther), a ruler (Tacitus). He is, after all, what his creator—man—would have him.

Emerson put it this way: "The god of the cannibals will be a cannibal, of the crusaders a crusader, and of the merchants a merchant." Goethe remonstrated: "As a man is, so is his God; therefore was God so often an object of mockery." As Voltaire wrote: "If God did not exist, it would be necessary to invent him"; which is precisely what Plato concluded in *Sisyphus:* "He was a wise man who invented God."

God—whether loved, feared, or respected—became a kind of last resort for humanity under pressure. From this general and widespread conclusion derived the custom of praying to Him, especially in adversity. The anthropologist Robert R. Marett explains: "Only if the deity be regarded as altogether superior is there room for prayer proper, that is, reverent entreaty." He also concedes that a "higher type" of prayer is "accompanied with disinterested homage, praise, and thanksgiving" but a "lower type" involves "on the one hand self-abasement, with confession of sins and promises of repentance and reform, or on the other hand, self-justification in the shape of the expression of faith and recitation of past services."

Marett cautions:

> If the worshiper place his god on a level with himself,
> so as to make him to some extent dependent on
> the service man contracts to render him,
> then genuine prayer tends to be replaced by a mere
> bargaining, often conjoined with flattery and
> insincere promises. . . . when high gods are kind
> for a consideration, the lower deities will likewise be
> found addicted to such commerce.

There is indeed an extraordinary legacy of this commercial kind of prayer in which God's human

clients either promise to render Him services
(a certain number of stanzas of theological mumbo
jumbo, according to the religious faith of the suppli-
cant; the promise of a geographical pilgrimage
[Mecca or Jerusalem or Rome], a financial offering,
or even a vow to build the Lord—or his designated
saint—a new private church).

The last-mentioned technique in the employment
for man's benefit of the God-man relationship is notable
in Greece, where a personalized view of divinity has
prevailed since before the invention of Zeus. Greek
islands are customarily made yet more beautiful by the
dozens of small churches they feature, whitewashed
tokens of gratitude from sailors who, threatened by
drowning in storms, invoked divine aid in exchange for
specific promises of architectural payment.

The most simple and therefore most touching
type of such prayer, offering divinity some kind
of exchange that may at least appear fair to the
donor (on the La Hire-Astley-Anhalt-Dessau basis),
is that propounded by or affecting children. One
from a Polynesian tribe:

> Big rat! little rat!
> Here is my old tooth.
> Pray give me a new one.
>
> *Rarotonga prayer (as
> child loses tooth)*

A similar—if far more bloodcurdling—tale is
told in the warlike Balkans. In this Serbian version,
the plea is made by a Bulgarian. In the precisely
reversed Bulgarian version, it is made by a Serb.

In either case, God is offered what is considered a square deal—a bizarre formula—even when the Lord is doing an unsolicited favor to his servant who, thus, has bitter supplication forced upon him. The story goes:

> Ivan Ivanov, the faithful Bulgarian peasant, earned his reward from God. God said to him: "Ivan, my son, you have been so fine a peasant that I shall honor you by doing anything you want. Only remember, in the name of generosity, whatever I do for you, I shall do twice as much for your neighbor across the river, Jovan Jovanović, the Serb." Ivan thought a while, removed his sheepskin cap and scratched his head. "Lord," said he, "so be it. Cut off one of my balls."
>
> *Serbian tale*

What the All-Merciful would be expected to do in exchange for services rendered with a Cook Islander's tooth or an odd set of southern Slavic testicles is, it would seem, not taken into consideration.

Another and well-known species of prayer for special favors, at least somewhat more dignified, does not presume to offer bargain-basement prices in exchange. God is simply addressed in his all-puissant capacity, not diminished or tarnished by the suggestion of a bribe.

Among these my favorite is the following, which is both more humorous and more deeply touching when it is remembered that the young cutup of a North African town who thus addressed his Divinity subsequently became one of the most esteemed, most holy, and most intellectual pillars of the Christian dogma. His immense religious influence is still today very much alive. The prayer was unadorned, abrupt:

> Oh God, make me good, but not yet.
>
> *St. Augustine (in his youth)*

A most agreeable and human entreaty to Heaven has been found below the inscription on an English tomb:

> Give me a sense of humor, Lord,
> Give me the grace to see a joke,
> To get some happiness from life
> And pass it on to other folk.
>
> *Anonymous (from a tablet in Chester Cathedral, England)*

The definition of prayer itself is complex. It is not necessarily related to religion or the concept of divinity. Fortune, the crapshooter's symbol of benevolence, is frequently beseeched for aid:

> Luck, be a lady tonight.
>
> *Frank Loesser*
> Guys and Dolls

> Seven, seven, come eleven.
>
> *Crapshooter's prayer*

The roster of special entreaties addressed by man to his invention, God, ranges from the ridiculous to the sublime. Thus we find a revered Greek Orthodox saint who, as a Russian-born soldier, was captured by troops of a Moslem Turkish officer and enslaved. He later requested his own Christian God to take care of a culinary favor for his owner, then on pilgrimage in Mecca, by sending him a homemade pilaf:

> O you who once in Babylon, answering the prayers
> of the prophet Abbakum, brought invisible food to
> Daniel in the lion's den, please answer my prayer too
> and send this food to my master in Mecca.

> *St. John of Cappadocia (when the
> slave of a Turkish officer)*

I cannot refrain from recalling of this particular Saint John, whose remains are now exposed in a pretentious little church on the Greek island of Evvoia, that his body was kidnapped by his admirers. John had been buried in a Greek village on the Turkish Anatolian coast. It was considered so holy and therefore so valuable that bits had been cut off and sold to wealthy, jealous Orthodox monasteries on the peninsula of Mount Athos. Posthumous sacrifice on behalf of his clients cost John a hand and foot. This can still be confirmed today by regarding the remains of his leathery corpse carefully exposed under glass.

When Turkey defeated the Greeks in 1922, the latter were expelled to Evvoia under a massive population exchange, and felt at a loss without their patron saint. So an expedition was sent by caique to Turkey. The men who volunteered for this undertaking deliberately fed strong drinks to the Moslems who had taken over their village. Then, when the Turks had succumbed to the powerful raki, the Greeks stole Saint John's battered remains, hid them under a cargo of coal in the hold of

their little boat, and sailed back to Evvoia. There he
was encased in a proud new church.

When Ishtar, chief goddess of Babylon and Assyria,
closely related to the latterday Venus, descended
to the underworld, her divine conversations were
largely limited to food:

> "What wilt thou give me for my food?
> What wilt thou give me for my sucking?"
> "I shall give thee the ripe fig,
> And the apricot."
> "Of what use are they to me, the ripe fig,
> And the apricot?
> Lift me up among the teeth,
> And among the gums cause me to dwell.
> The blood of the tooth I will suck,
> And of the gum I will gnaw its roots."

> *Ishtar's Descent to the Underworld*
> *(Babylonian)*

In the warm, windswept Scilly Islands, west
of Britain and famed at various times in history
for its pillagers, its daffodils, and the presence of
that modest golfer, the vacationing Harold Wilson,
a traditional prayer goes:

> We pray Thee, Oh Lord, that if wrecks
> will happen,
> Thou wilt guide them into the Scilly Isles.

> *Old Scilly prayer*

They tell the tale in the Scillies of a parson
whose Sunday sermon was interrupted by a cry of
"wreck" and how he hollered, as his greedy congregation leaped to its feet: "One moment, my
friends, let us start fair."

This same cruel hope that others' ill fortune may benefit the impoverished inhabitants of a bleak and isolated isle is not limited to the off-shore spits of Cornwall. Far, far to the south the young women of a dreary and inhospitable rock, with slight chance of dowry produced by any normal effort, beg of their deity:

> Please God send me a wreck, that I may marry.
>
> *Tristan da Cunha (girl's prayer)*

The antebellum Kentuckians, a lusty, hardy breed, had their own special plea (bespoken most frequently outside church and to the tinkle of mint juleps rather than the sonority of hymns):

> May you live to be a hundred, and then
> be hanged for rape.
>
> *Kentucky toast*

Avarice is an ancient human weakness, and it appears again and again among the recorded yearnings of our species, as for example:

> Let me be called the worst of mankind
> so long as I am called rich.
>
> *Latin proverb*

Likewise, safety—whether from human transgressors or from natural happenings—is a frequent subject of prayer. Thus:

> Kiss the hand you dare not bribe,
> and pray for its destruction.
>
> *Old Arab proverb*

And also, on a gentler, nobler note:

> O Great Spirit!
> Thou hast made this lake;
> Thou hast also created us as Thy children;
> Thou art able to make this water calm
> Until we have safely passed over.

Chippewa Voyager's Prayer

Broadly speaking, it is my conclusion, after studying the texts of hundreds of prayers from many regions and which traverse a broad span of time, that those seeking special favor or comfort can be divided into two categories: the frank, practical plea and the intellectual or sensuous expression of greater (often spiritual) needs.

Practicality is in no sense sinful. Even such mystics as St. Teresa were convinced of its intrinsic worth. Time and again this unexpected note creeps into her devotions as when, somewhat wryly, she begs the stern Lord whom she passionately adores:

> From foolish devotions may God deliver us.

St. Teresa of Avila

How similar is the mood of the greatest Athenian statesman who asks his divine mentors:

> Grant that no word may fall from me
> against my will unfit for the present need.

Pericles

The seventeenth century's most famous victim of regicide addressed what he himself recognized was perforce a prayer and no longer a command to the

masked headsman waiting beside him at the block,
saying to the executioner:

> Have a care of the axe. . . . I pray you, do not put me
> to pain. . . . I shall say but a short prayer and, when I
> hold out my hands thus, strike.

> *King Charles I*

But throughout the ages we have had far less grim
requests for pleasant help from men preoccupied
with life's agreeable aspects. Thus:

> At the beginning of the cask and at the end take thy
> fill, but be saving in the middle; for at the bottom
> saving comes too late.

> *Hesiod*

The youthful poet Keats saw in wine its relationship
to life and song and music, craving:

> O for a draught of vintage! that hath been
> Cool'd a long age in the deep-delvèd earth. . . .
> O for a beaker full of the warm South . . .
> That I might drink, and leave the world unseen,
> And with thee fade away. . . .

> *John Keats, "Ode to a Nightingale"*

And yet, curiously, the profound and intellectual
Augustine, one of the church's greatest fathers,
was forced by his honesty to confess (as suited one
whose earlier days strayed from the narrow path of
holiness):

> Drunkenness is far from me; Thou wilt grant
> in Thy mercy that it never approach me;
> but gluttony sometimes steals upon Thy servant.

> *St. Augustine*

Another saint was so well known for the assistance he rendered his particular clientele, those who worked with leather to earn their keep, that they devised to him this special request:

Dear Saint, the saint of those who make good shoes,
Thee for my patron saint I also choose.
Whene'er I walk in highway, trail or street,
Bring thou unblistered home my grateful feet.

*Prayer to St. Crispin (patron of
shoemakers and tanners)*

Often it has been conceded by modest thoughtful men that divinity, whatever its attributes, should clearly be wiser than humanity. This benefit of judgment is conceded to the gods from earliest days, accordingly:

King Zeus, grant us the good whether we pray for it
or not, but evil keep from us though we pray for it.

Plato

Almost precisely the same thought was expressed more than two thousand years later by François de Fénelon, the seventeenth-century archbishop of Cambrai, a brilliant writer and aristocratic theologian. He asked only:

O Father, give to us, thy children,
that which we ourselves know not how to ask.

François Fénelon

By indirection, a celebrated twentieth-century English Catholic author arrived at a similar desire:

Take not Thy thunder from us
But take away our pride!

Gilbert Keith Chesterton

God was often regarded as a personal ally against
the vicissitudes of life and fortune. One pragmatic
Briton was especially inclined to this hopeful view,
in such instances as:

Merciful and loving Father,
We beseech thee most humbly, even with all our
hearts, to pour out upon our enemies with
bountiful hands, whatsoever things thou
knowest will do them good.

Sixteenth-century prayer

This eminently sensible approach marks English
relations with divinity again and again. The eighteenth-
century clergyman John Wesley, who migrated to
America and taught his own brand of Methodism,
begged:

O Lord, let us not live to be useless;
for Christ's sake. AMEN.

John Wesley

And even Charles Lamb, in no sense a cleric, wanted
only this:

I ask and wish not to appear
More beauteous, rich or gay:
Lord, make me wiser every year,
And better every day.

Charles Lamb

Some of the favors asked from all expressions of God—ranging between Catholic, Protestant, and the American Indian's Great Spirit—were endearing and lovely as well as clearly practical. A famous Augustinian canon who dwelt in Holland during the later Middle Ages suggested:

> Who can tell what a day may bring forth?
> Cause us, therefore, gracious God, to live every day
> as if it were to be our last, for that we know not
> but it may be such.
>
> *Thomas à Kempis*

The Apaches, far more philosophical and kindly than the propaganda of an official U. S. enemy allowed during its nineteenth-century war of expropriation and extermination, intoned reverently:

> Stenatleha, you are good, I pray for long life.
> I pray for your good looks.
> I pray for good breath.
> I pray for good speech.
> I pray for feet like yours to carry me
>   through a long life.
> I pray for a life like yours.
> I walk with people; ahead of me all is well.
> I pray for people to smile as long as I live.
> I pray to live long.
>
> *Apache Medicine Song*

The father of Thomism gently begged:

> Thou Who makest eloquent the tongues of
> little children, fashion my words and pour upon
> my lips the grace of Thy benediction. Grant me
> penetration to understand, capacity to retain,

method and facility in study, subtlety in
interpretation and abundant grace of expression.

St. Thomas Aquinas

Stern, self-denying (if on occasion gently whimsical),
the great Teresa asked of God only to furnish the
strength she needed to serve Him:

If Thou wilt [prove me] by means of trials,
give me strength and let them come.

St. Teresa of Avila

And the Protestant reformer whose influence spread
in France during its religious wars echoed this plea—
but clearly reckoning more on the Lord's strength than
his own:

Defend us in soul and body from all harm.
Guard us against the assaults of the devil
and deliver us from any danger that may beset us.

John Calvin

*(Admiral Coligny, the Huguenot leader, was
saying this prayer with his chaplain on the
morning of St. Bartholomew's Day, 1572, when
assassins broke into his room and murdered
him.)*

Another—not saint but poet laureate, a time-serving
profession—had (as a seafarer, sea-worshiper must have)
a direct, clear-skied view of divinity, and asked this fate:

Grant the last prayer that I shall pray,
    Be good to me, O Lord!

And let me pass in a night at sea, a night
    of storm and thunder,
In the loud crying of the wind through
    sail and rope and spar;

> Send me a ninth great peaceful wave to
>   drown and roll me under
> To the cold tunny-fishes' home where the
>   drowned galleons are.

John Masefield

A very devout and very simple Catholic sister had a profoundly intuitive vision of the order of things, with special tenderness for the lesser creatures. She reminded:

> Do not forget, Lord,
> it is I who make the sun rise.
> I am Your servant
> but, with the dignity of my calling,
> I need some glitter and ostentation.

Carmen Bernos de Gasztold
"Cock's Prayer"

And a wise, realistic Scotsman limited his own request to this (despite the illness that was to plague him for so many years):

> Lord, give us to go blithely on our business all this day, bring us to our resting beds weary and content and undishonored, and grant us in the end the gift of sleep.

Robert Louis Stevenson

The miserable Stuart heiress, foolish but devout, who had more reason than most to pray, asked helplessly of God before her tragic death:

> O Lord my God, I hope in thee;
> My dear Lord Jesus, set me free;
> In chains, in pains,

I long for thee.
On bended knee.
I adore thee, implore thee
To set me free.

Mary Queen of Scots (in prison)

Edwin Markham, with somewhat excessive natur-
alism, pleaded with God:

Teach me, Father, how to be
Kind and patient as a tree.

Edwin Markham

Thoreau, philosopher of the New England backwoods,
didn't ask but simply thanked his stars for a favor
already accorded him, protection against the journalists
(of whom I am one) who plague our contemporary
world:

Blessed are they who never read a newspaper,
for they shall see Nature, and, through her, God.

Henry David Thoreau
Essays and Other Writings

And, to terminate this additional chapter of uncommon prayers, the words of Hafiz, written by himself for his own tomb:

O thou who passeth by my tomb, ask a favor,
For here will be the shrine of the *rènds** of this world!

Tomb of Hafiz, Iran

---

* Persian word meaning a special one whose exterior acts are
blameworthy but who is inwardly upright.

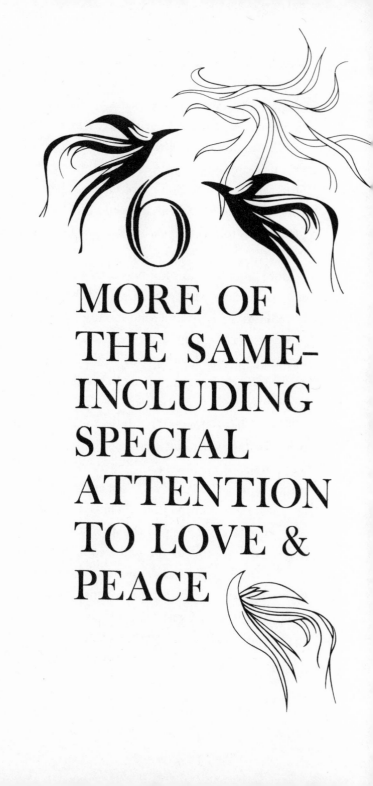

6

MORE OF THE SAME- INCLUDING SPECIAL ATTENTION TO LOVE & PEACE

Man has long been familiar with various types of prayer. Some are accompanied by secret words or magic spells supposed to add efficacy. Plato mentioned the eagerness of early Greeks to talk with their gods. But many of those who entreat for divine help are not precisely sure what they wish. In Orissa the Indian Khond people address their deity with open minds: "We are ignorant of what it is good to ask for. You know what is good for us. Give it to us."

More usual than this kind of tolerance, which presupposes greater wisdom than many believers seem to credit to the Lord, is a kind of bullying approach to the question of divine succor; a "positive hectoring" is how Marett describes the process when applied in primitive places, "with dictation, threats, and abuse.

"Even," he continues, "the Italian peasant is said occasionally to offer both abuse and physical violence to the image of a recalcitrant saint." The anthropologist mentions a "conditional curse" applied to recalcitrant or uncooperative saints in Morocco, and the Zulu's warning to the ancestral ghost he worships: "Help me or you will feed on nettles."

Some theologians consider prayer the core of religion. It surely derives from crude incantations of proto-witch doctors; yet the inspiration obviously stems from an instinct to wish, whether for one's own good fortune or the ill fortune of an enemy or rival.

Prayers can, of course, have negative intent. In either case, positive or negative, they require the assumption that the being supplicated is powerful and (hopefully) well disposed. Most primitive prayers sought only alleviation of worldly ills or improvement of one's lot. However, as religion became more intricate, so did the aspirations expressed by praying.

For me, the prayers of joy are among man's most beautiful creations, as are some of those delightfully human religionaries who uttered them: Dame Juliana Berners, a holy and trout-fly-tying abbess-angler; Saint Chrisopher Kynokephalos, the handsome lad who romped with the girls until a hard-hearted God, leaning over the gold bar of heaven, turned his handsome head into a dog's, driving him to sanctity; Saint Francis, also a youthful rake, whose adoration of the flowers, birds, and beasts is still commemorated at Assisi in Christendom's gayest church; and Saint Augustine, that wise African scholar who, as a young man, could beseech God not to make him good too soon; or even, for that matter, Mary Magdalene, who showed that a saint's clean mind can tenant the battered body of a whore.

Sheer exuberant joy of being is reflected in many sweet prayers quite as strongly as fear of quitting this existence echoes directly or indirectly in others, more timorous if equally tender. Happy or frightened, earthy or spiritual, simple or profound, the odd mélange of prayers herewith presented from the corners of the earth and the recesses of time have this in common: a certain quality of goodness.

What, for example, could be more pure than this poetic ecstasy of an ethereal and gifted, if poor and pallid, always sickly mid-Victorian lady:

> As the wind is thy symbol,
> So forward our goings.
> As the dove,
> So launch us heavenwards.
> As water,
> So purify our spirits.
> As a cloud,
> So abate our temptations.
> As dew,
> So revive our languor.
> As fire,
> So purge out our dross.
>
> *Christina Rossetti*

John Donne, death-obsessed dean of St. Paul's who is hard to recognize in the young Elizabethan poet, is one of the great geniuses of seventeenth-century England. As a youthful Catholic man of fashion, and a roisterer, he wrote some of the loveliest poems of all time—and even in them one can recognize the intellectual developments that would lead him to the pulpit and to fame as a frightening, and frighteningly intellectual, sermonist.

He changed both career and religion when the aristocratic family into which he married blocked his advancement because of his Catholicism. His wife presented him with several children so, in the end, he took orders in his new Anglican faith, thus assuring his family the economic support of a different church. He also assured himself of a brand new role in literature's eternity.

Can one not detect this twinned aspect of his genius in the following early love poem, when he thought more of the delights of God's expression on earth (through a pretty woman) than of the austere, eternal passages of endlessness he later came to contemplate so bleakly:

> For Godsake hold your tongue, and let me love,
> Or chide my palsie, or my gout,
> My five gray haires, or ruin'd fortune flout,
> With wealth your state, your minde with Arts
>   improve,
> Take you a course, get you a place,
> Observe his honour, or his grace,
> Or the Kings reall, or his stamped face
> Contemplate, what you will, approve,
> So you will let me love.
>
> *John Donne*

Contrast this complex intellectualization of carnal delight with the simple peasant reality of formalized sainthood (enrolled in the religion Donne forsook):

> Lord, I desire that, at all times, those who profit
> by my labor may be not only refreshed in body,
> but may be also drawn to Thy love and
> strengthened in every good.
>
> *A Cook's Prayer (St. Gertrude and
> St. Mechtilde)*

Or a well-known Czechoslovakian playwright, best regarded as a satirist of man's onrushing future

state, but (as one sees here) a truly simple individual
with his feet rooted deeply in the soil:

> O Lord, grant that in some way it may rain every day,
> say from about midnight until three o'clock in
> the morning. . . . gentle and warm so that it
> can soak in . . . that there may be plenty of dew
> and little wind, enough worms, no plant-lice and snails,
> no mildew, and that once a week thin liquid manure
> and guano may fall from heaven.

> *Karel Čapek "The Gardener's Prayer"*
> *(1931)*

Unusual and delicate favors are often asked of God
by man. Socrates' most famous student places these
words in the mouth of his peerless master:

> Socrates: "O beloved Pan and all ye other gods
> of this place, grant to me that I be made beautiful
> in my soul within, and that all external possessions
> be in harmony with my inner man. May I consider the
> wise man rich; and may I have such wealth as
> only the self-restrained man can endure.
> Do we need anything more, Phaedrus?
> For me that prayer is enough."

> *Plato* Phaedrus

The greatest of the sixteenth-century artist-giants,
that baroque tower who bullied even popes, known
less for his fine poetry than his tactile genius, asked
only of his Maker:

> Do thou, then, breathe those thoughts into my mind
> By which such virtue may in me be bred
> That in thy holy footsteps I may tread:
> The fetters of my tongue do thou unbend,

That I may have the power to sing of thee
And sound thy praises everlastingly.

Michaelangelo

The gentlest saint who, I suspect, adored his dumb
brethren even more than those who could express
their wants, requested for them:

> Have pity, O Lord God, lest they who go by the way
> trample on the unfledged bird, and send thine Angel to
> replace it in the nest, that it may live till it can fly.

St. Augustine

His martial colleague on the canonical list, a man
who organized legions to conquer body as well as
soul in the name of Christ, spoke like a good officer
when he somewhat arbitrarily demanded:

> Teach us, good Lord, to serve Thee
>   as Thou deservest:
> To give and not to count the cost;
> To fight and not to heed the wounds;
> To toil and not to seek for rest;
> To labor and not ask for any reward
> Save that of knowing that we do Thy will.

St. Ignatius Loyola

An Indian sage, whose sanctity would surely have
been formalized had he been a Westerner living at
the right time and adhering to the right creed,
thought soulfully:

> O master poet, I have sat down at thy feet.
> Only let me make my life simple and straight,
> like a flute of reed for thee to fill with music.

Rabindranath Tagore

The last epoch of France's Renaissance can boast of two playwright-poets (Racine and Corneille) who, combined together, might have equaled Shakespeare. Of these one wrote with felicitous practicality a special kind of prayer:

> Puisse le Ciel
> Verser sur toutes vos Années
> Mille prospérités
> l'une à l'autre enchaînées.
>
> *Racine*

Those of us familiar with the Bible sometimes forget the extraordinary Epicurean character of the great king of Jerusalem who, although famed for his sagacity and his monuments, was very much of the "gather-ye-rosebuds-while-ye-may" school of the French Pléiade and the English Renaissance. Indeed, he said it better, and if his is not a prayer, it is certainly a credo:

> Let us enjoy the good things that are present,
> and let us speedily use the creatures like as in youth.
> Let us fill ourselves with costly wine and ointments;
> and let no flower of the spring pass by us.
> Let us crown ourselves with rosebuds before they
> be withered; let none of us go without his part
> of our voluptuousness, let us leave tokens of our
> joyfulness in every place; for this is our portion,
> and our lot is this.
>
> *The Wisdom of Solomon*

A more visionary man, infinitely more mystical than the cunning and grandiose Hebrew ruler ever could have been, a desperate English poet-painter begged:

> O Savior, pour upon me thy spirit of meekness and love,
> annihilate the Selfhood in me, be thou all my life.
> Guide thou my hand which trembles exceedingly
> upon the rock of ages.
>
> *William Blake*

The divine respect or aid solicited of divinity by the ancient world was curiously mixed between arrogant vanity, adoration, eloquence, and fear. The namesake of this writer commanded (to all gods and all men):

> I am Cyrus, king of the world, great king,
> legitimate king, king of Babylon, king of Sumer
> and Akkad, king of the four rims [of the earth]. . . .
> May all the gods whom I have resettled in their
> sacred cities ask daily Bel and Nebo for a long life
> for me and may they recommend me [to him];
> to Marduk, my lord, they may say this:
> "Cyrus, the king who worships you, and Cambyses,
> his son . . ." . . . all of them I settled in a peaceful
> place . . . ducks and doves . . . I endeavoured to
> fortify/repair their dwelling places. . . .
>
> *Inscription on a clay barrel, Iran*

How vividly this contrasts with the even earlier acceptance, in an even older civilization, of man's relation to the universe around him:

> Thou savest the silent, O Thou,
> Thou sweet well of water for him
>   who is athirst in the desert!
> It is closed for the eloquent;

It is open for the silent.
When the silent cometh, he findeth the well;
The one that burneth with heat, him dost
    Thou refresh.

Egyptian papyrus

That was pagan Egypt—pagan, but curiously more tender and less pompous than that brief interruption sponsored by priests of Amen, the monotheistic god of gods, and brought in by priests of Akhenaten and his eternally beautiful queen Nefertiti. These rulers boasted of their short-lived dynasty:

Son of the Sun, living in truth,
The Lord of diadems, Akh-en-aten.
Long [be] his life,
And the chief royal wife, beloved of him,
    the mistress of both countries,
Nefer-nefru-aten, Nefert-iti,
Who liveth and flourisheth for ever
    and for eternity.

Amenhotep IV "Hymn to the Sun"

In Canaan, the Promised Land whose rule was usurped by a fierce, desert-trained Jewish army that had fled Egypt under Moses' leadership, prayer proved frustrating. Witness:

Ask life, O hero Aqht
Ask life and I will give it thee,
Immortality and I will freely grant it thee.
I will make thee number years with Baal,
Even with the sons of El wilt thou tell months.
As Baal, even as he lives and is feted,
Lives and is feted and they give him to drink,

> Singing and chanting before him,
> Singing of him, even the Gracious One,
> Even so will I give thee life, O hero Aqht.

Legend of King Dn'il (Canaan)

We are told of Gilgamesh, hero of Babylonia and king of the first dynasty of Erech, who ruled 126 years (in those glorious days!), who survived the flood, and had direct contact with several gods and goddesses, that even he cowered before death and needed reassurance:

> Only the gods live forever under the sun.
> As for mankind, numbered are their days;
> Whatever they achieve is but wind!
> Even here thou art afraid of death.
> What of thy heroic might?

Babylonian tablet

This awareness of mortality is echoed in a great lord of Japan whose touching quatrain pleads:

> If I should come no more,
> Plum-tree beside my door,
> Forget not thou the spring,
> Faithfully blossoming.

*Shogun Minamoto Sanetomo
(composed the morning before his
assassination in 1219)*

Because of this awareness, the best among men have craved of God, if anything, the strength always to survive well a brief incarnation and to bring happiness thereby to others. Thus, once again, Francis:

Lord, make me an instrument of thy peace!
Where there is hatred . . . let me sow love.
Where there is injury . . . pardon.
Where there is doubt . . . faith.
Where there is despair . . . hope.
Where there is darkness . . . light.
Where there is sadness . . . joy.

St. Francis of Assisi

And finally that pious Boeotian, Pindar, notable for his religiosity, asked divinity in a deathless ode:

May I walk, O God, in the guileless paths of life, and leave behind me a fair name for my children. O God, that bringest all things to pass, grant me the spirit of reverence for noble things.

Pindar

7

OF
DESPAIR
& FOR
MERCY

For mankind, God was first an expression of awe, then of faith; and finally the consequent poetry was supported by a complex structure of inadequate logic. Now the remnants of this theological architecture are forced to lean almost solely on the first pillar, faith, by a kind of extrasensory perception of which belief in God is the ultimate expression.

But this reliance on divinity remains psychologically essential to most men, habituated to dependence by ancient custom. God has become the excuse for all our mistakes, and religion is the substitute for our ignorance. To rephrase Descartes, we think we know, therefore we imagine we are.

First we worshipped rocks on a flat earth and stars flickering over its dishlike surface. When we found substitutes for rocks and discovered the world was round, we simply shifted the objects of our adoration. But we still insist there must be God because who else could begin or end things?

We fail to acknowledge one implication that might be read into J.B.S. Haldane: What if, in a universe "queerer than we *can* suppose," both beginning and end are ridiculous nonexistent terms?

Suppose we accept the possibility that a tiny atom in a man's body is as important to that body as is the man himself to Earth. Then, maybe, Earth is even less important to the galaxy it inhabits than is the atom to the individual's body. And there are galaxies each in size beyond our ability to contemplate; also, these galaxies are endless in number and in the space they occupy.

Yet as this vague idea of outward-expanding infinity is digested, can we also imagine a similar infinity endlessly expanding inward: from man's body to that single atom, and from that atom again inward to something smaller than the tiniest microcosm ever yet conceived, and so on? And when this thought is entertained, we find that same atom as anonymous and unimportant to our galaxy as is William Shakespeare to its neighbor, some billions of light-years off.

You are as anonymous and unimportant to the dead planet Saturn as a compendium of Moses, Jesus, Mohammed, and the Buddha is significant to other galaxies not yet detected on the finest spatial telescope. All this world's intellectual history would weigh as a feather on the planet Mercury. Obsessed by life, as distinct from the wholly inanimate, what similarity can we observe between algae and apes, or ferns and frogs?

Our ultimately comforting religious concepts, first tabulated by medieval Thomism, were again intellectualized during the seventeenth century of Reformation and Counter-Reformation thought and counterthought. Descartes wrote: "There is nothing so far removed from us as to be beyond our reach or so hidden that we cannot discover it." This is delightfully assuring. But is it true?

Even if we know that a spoonful of the material comprising a neutron star (one of which has yet to be discovered) would weigh one billion tons and, at that density, our earth would be barely a hundred yards in diameter, what bottomless pits of additional knowledge remain to be tasted before we revise theology itself? Is the final logic this: Post-Nietzsche man must kill God because pre-Nietzsche man invented him?

As an atheist, I am convinced of my negativism, although I underline my reluctance to win anyone to my credo. I also bless those who believe in anything, for their ability to believe. But, although a nonbeliever, I have faith in the creed of beauty. In such terms maybe mankind's invention of God was his most beautiful creation; certainly it was his most poignant.

Nor is conformity in an idea of God requisite to prayer. Buddhism has no God; Christianity has, as it were, three Gods in one; Hinduism has a plethora of Gods believing in neither a beginning nor an end. The Jews had a frightening but just God, although in time He became slightly less harsh and more merciful.

The only connection between these intellectual approaches is that all the world's great religions evolved in Asia. Also, one might add, they all tend to obscure mythology when analyzed. Perhaps they follow the old Jewish proverb: "Be obscure that you may endure."

And each divinity serves as the accustomed recipient of prayers from its priesthood or its flock or both, whether the pitiful papered prayer wheels of Tibetan Buddhist practitioners, the reverent and healthy bowing of Moslems facing Mecca, or the silent, wordless murmuring of Zen priests seeing nothing in concrete objects. This purely mystical aspect of prayer is especially appealing.

It is possible to list prayers that are not addressed to divinity, as, for example, the superstitionist's plea for aid and protection. But there is another kind of wholly impractical prayer or pseudo-prayer, which is the sheer ecstasy of beauty for beauty's sake.

Moreover, it is astonishing how often this particular form is best expressed by believers, by practicants of one or another creed, from the authors of Old Testament Psalms to the lovely writings of St. Francis of Assisi and St. John of the Cross, or the genial Father Gerard Manley Hopkins.

Here one must include the old Irish poem: "The speckled fish leaps, Strong is the bond of the swift warrior."

There is no reason whatsoever that prayer must be confined to begging favors—even if one believes there exists a superior being who will heed him— or to extreme pleas for mercy on life's ultimate thresholds. It is one of history's weirdest aspects of illogic, indeed, that man should pray for the most part to the greatest creature of his own invention, God, in order to avoid the menace of his own creation, death.

That great dean of St. Paul's, John Donne, who took religious orders because he could find no other satisfactory trade, suggested: "The devil is overcome by resisting, but the world and the flesh by running away."

What we cannot escape is the hell of death's final anonymity which, once we had invented the limbo that preceded life, our sense of order imposed relentlessly upon us. The very thought of such an eternal and implacable condition suggests an agony transcending the most exquisite of pains:

"The dark night and dry purgation of the desire," as St. John of the Cross described it; one that his fellow Spaniard, St. Teresa of Avila, approached as she died, with a final, fearful cry to God: "A broken and a contrite heart. Thou wilt not despise." So recollecting, I, the atheist, close this prolegomenon with words from Thomas More, also regarded as a heretic in his time: "The things, good Lord, that I pray for, give me Thy grace to labor for. Amen."

The most desperate of all prayers, if such it may be called, is that of Christ upon the cross. It is not a prayer and only inferentially a plea. But it is infinite in its bewilderment and bewildering in the infinity of its meaning.

How, one asks, can the concept of God, an integral portion of that illogical theorem, the Holy Trinity, pray to God (which means therefore to Himself) complaining he has been forsaken? And if forsaken, by whom and why?

When one recalls the mystery of the Resurrection, one wonders why this form of suffering was accepted by its victim, then why that victim complained after having, as it would seem, imposed the suffering upon himself. And in the end, why is this misery considered by theology to be necessary

for mankind's uplifting and purification? It does
indeed require faith to follow this thought, but then,
as I have said earlier, faith is for me an indifferent
substitute for reason and a poor pretense for understanding.

As the faithful evangelist recalls of this extraordinary drama:

> And about the ninth hour Jesus cried with a loud voice,
> "Eli, Eli, la'ma Sabach-thá-ni?",
> that is,
> "My God, my God, why hast Thou forsaken me?"
>
> *Matthew*

In the unforgettable shadow of this misery many
holy followers of Christ have meekly acknowledged,
as implicitly did the Son of God, that they could not
face the ultimate tests that might be put to them.
Not all saints are at the same time heroes; some are
simply good. Thus, for example:

> O Lord, put no trust in me; for I shall surely fail
> if thou uphold me not.
>
> *St. Philippo de Neri*

Oddly enough, that medieval Himalayan sage,
Milarepa, in his eagle's nest, began his own most
excruciating appeal with precisely the same words
as did St. Philippo:

> O Lord, Embodiment of the Eternal Buddhas,
> Thou Refuge of all Sentient Creatures,
> Out of the depths of Thy Great Love and Wisdom
> Hearest Thou the lamentation of Thy
>   Suppliant Unfortunate,
> Rechung-Dorje-Tagpa?

Unto Thee, in misery and woe, I cry;
If Thou wilt not Thy Love and Wisdom now
exert
To shield Thy Son, for whom else shouldst
Thou, Lord? . . .

Exert Thy Kindness, grant Thy Grace, O Father.

Yogi Milarepa of Tibet

Many are those who, on behalf of other humans, have called upon God to witness generous acts. Abraham Lincoln, a sad, wise, homespun, and deeply sympathetic president, asked:

I pray that our Heavenly Father may assuage·the anguish of your bereavement, and leave you only the cherished memory of the loved and lost, and the solemn pride that must be yours, to have laid so costly a sacrifice upon the altar of Freedom.

Abraham Lincoln

In the liturgy of St. Mark it is written:

We must earnestly beseech thee, O thou Lover of mankind, to look in thy mercy upon all prisoners.

Liturgy of St. Mark

During the sixteenth century there was a widely known prayer for political prisoners (something that might well have been revived and multiplied during all ensuing years):

Be merciful, O Father of all mercies, to such as are under persecution for the testimony of their conscience.

Anonymous (prayer for political prisoners, 1585)

And the Pope who saw his own flock torn apart during World War I begged his God, in puzzlement (and without success):

> Inspire rulers and peoples with counsels of meekness.
> Heal the discords that tear nations asunder.
> Thou Who didst shed Thy precious blood that
> they might live as brothers, bring men together once
> more in loving harmony. To the cry of the
> Apostle Peter: "Save us, Lord, we perish,"
> Thou didst answer words of mercy and didst still
> the raging waves. Deign now to hear our trustful
> prayers and give back to the world order and peace.

Pope Benedict XV (1854–1922)

One who vigorously and with great earnestness asked God's help was that religious revolutionist who, standing up against an earlier pope's man, proclaimed:

> I cannot and I will not retract. Here I stand,
> I can do no other. May God help me! AMEN.

*Martin Luther (to the Diet of
Worms, 1521)*

This plea for aid and sustenance is echoed by many faithful, strong, devout people throughout time. As it is well expressed:

> Thou who didst spread thy creating arms to the stars,
> strengthen our arms with power to intercede
> when we lift up our hands unto thee.

Armenian liturgy

And how often the clean and generous man asks divine help to purify those exemplary sentiments:

Heavenly King, Paraclete, Spirit of Truth,
present in all places and filling all things,
Treasury of good and Choir-master of life:
come and dwell within us, cleanse us from all stains
and save our souls.

St. John Chrysostom

A famous modern Jesuit, Sinologue and Orientalist, acquainted with much of the East's wisdom, prayed:

Savior of human suffering to which You have given
living value, be also the Savior of human unity;
compel us to discard our pettinesses, and to venture
forth, resting upon you, into the undaunted ocean
of charity.

Pierre Teilhard de Chardin

While it is rarely so expressed, it seems to me that loneliness is an implicit theme in the prayer relationship between man and the God he has created to assuage his thirst for company. In the words of one early martyr:

Take away from me the heart of stone, and give me a
heart of flesh, a heart to love and adore Thee,
a heart to delight in Thee, to follow and to enjoy Thee,
for Christ's sake.

St. Ambrose

Even the controlled Spanish feminist wailed:

Oh, God help me! What a miserable life is this!
There is no happiness that is secure and nothing that
does not change. . . . Oh, if only we thought
carefully about the things of life, we should each find
by experience how little either of happiness or of
unhappiness there is to be got from it!

St. Teresa of Avila

The Bishop of Hippo (here both mature and exceptionally good, as he had aspired eventually to be) asked:

> Watch Thou, dear Lord, with those who wake,
> or watch or weep tonight.

St. Augustine

Man's tininess and weakness in the eternal cosmogony often terrifies him; he seeks divine solace and inspiration:

> Remember, O Lord, my littleness; not the faults and
> ignorance of the past, but according to thy mercies,
> for if Thou take count of our iniquities,
> who shall abide it?

West Syrian liturgy

And peace, which man is doomed to have in death, he nevertheless seeks in life aboard this turbulent world:

> Lord, by thy divine silence, by thy wondrous patience,
> by thine adorable humility, keep me quiet and still,
> and possess me with thy peace.

Father Andrew

Prayers are mixed with yearning, and with pitiful confidence that they may achieve their expressed objective:

> O answer now the whisper of my prayer;
> Be gracious to my cry,
> Most holy God!

Jewish prayer

The genuine mystic, in order to facilitate understanding of his own aching needs, is able to put
himself, as it were, in his God's own shoes:

> What is it that afflicts thee, little sinner?
> Am I not thy God? Seest thou not how ill I am
> treated here? If thou lovest Me, why dost thou not
> grieve for Me?
>
> *St. Teresa of Avila*

God can be awarded the special chore of looking after
one's friends:

> Lord, bless Thy special friends and mine,
> according to the good pleasure of Thy divine goodness.
>
> *St. Gertrude and St. Mechtilde*

Yet for some, as Islam warns, He must be stern:

> Let not thy hand be tied up to thy neck;
> neither open it with an unbounded expansion,
> lest thou become worthy of reprehension, and be
> reduced to poverty.
>
> *The Koran*

The same source warns there can be no double-
dealing with God; He will have no truck with those
who seek to fool Him or neglect Him:

> Woe be unto those who pray, and who are negligent
> at their prayer: who play the hypocrites, and deny
> necessaries to the needy.
>
> *The Koran*

The Old Testament expresses its praise with a hint
of doubting skepticism:

> Praised be God who hath not cast out my prayer
> nor turned his mercy from me.   *Psalm 66*

A medieval French king begs for inspiration in all fields:

> Quench thou our passion's fire,
> Raise thou each low desire,
> Deeds of brave love inspire,
>   Quickener and Rest!

King Robert of France
(c. A.D. 1000)

Even an ancient father of the church fears our qualities may prove to have been insufficient, and he hopes for aid:

> Let our eyes pour forth floods of tears before we
> go hence, lest we fall into that place where tears
> will only increase the flames in which we shall burn.

St. Makarios the Elder

More than any people the Jews have reason to pray for an end to hatred:

> Cause hatred and strife to vanish,
> That abiding peace may fill the earth,
> And humanity may everywhere be blessed
>   with the fruits of peace.

Jewish prayer

Yet as that gentle figure Carmen Bernos de Gasztold reminds us, with Saint Francis, we must never forget our animal brethren:

> Hear our prayer, we beseech thee. For all beasts of
> burden, labor and toil in all the ways they go;
> touch their worn bodies; heal their wounds,
> ease their burdens, and strengthen their limbs.
> We pray for every man, woman, and child who goes
> with them—that thou wilt keep them from cruelty.

"Litany for the Animals"

But for all of us who live, thinking or unthinking, it is the same: we drift as thistledown and blow as evanescent spume:

> Do with me as Thou wilt; my will is Thy will;
> I appeal not against Thy judgments.

Epictetus

In the end, however, the greatest craving by frightened, doubting mankind of its God is a craving for mercy, for help and insurance that the infinite will be gentle, come what may, and regardless of inadequate preparation:

> May your heart, my god, cease to be grieved by me!
> The irate goddess, may her wrath be soon
>   appeased. . . .
> If my sins are many, make my guilt as nought;
> If my crimes are sevenfold, let your heart not
>   grieve;
> If my crimes are many, the greater your mercy be.

Lamentation to Quiet the Heart
(Sumerian)

8
DEIST
PRAYERS

Prayer is often a substitute for faith, which is itself a substitute for understanding. If one has true faith, why ask for its affirmation? Likewise, prayer can be a means of insuring against superstition, as it were a verbal form of knocking wood.

The rosary—which seemingly long antedates Christianity and which, in the eastern Mediterranean, is used to work off nervous energy with the fingers ("worry beads," they are called)—is another example.

But the rosary is not a form of, or replacement for, prayer. It is only connected with the latter when given a particular function, like keeping count of the number of lines or special pleas for reverence assigned by a priest or an individual conscience.

As the centuries spun past, most religions tended to develop an increased sophistication of expression, combined with a richness of presentation. This appealed to the sense of awe and also to the sense of beauty, music, and spectacle inherent in mankind. The actual method of entreaty was formalized in a definite methodology of prayer.

Particular postures were recommended (kneeling, prostrating), the hands held in special fashion (folded, clasped). The more complicated ways of praying are seen in major organized religions.

All advocate daily rites for specific individuals in addition to community worship. Many creeds also schedule fixed times to pray. The psychological approach varies: ritualistic, imposed by habit, aimed at escaping retribution, tinged with egoistic considerations ("Give us each day our daily bread").

There are, of course, exceptions. Buddhism knows a charming prayer: "May every living thing, movable or unmovable, tall, big or medium-sized, clumsy or refined, visible or invisible, near or far, already born or aspiring to birth—may all beings have a happy heart."

From systematic praying derived the idea of special prayers for special purposes. The ancient Jewish liturgy, "Seder Rab Amram," designated prayers for circumcision, for marriage, for travelers, for the Sabbath, for the New Moon.

This compilation served as the model for various subsequent liturgies. The most famous was that of the learned twelfth-century philosopher, Moses Maimonides, who worked out an elaborate program of prayer for the entire year.

The community spirit of religion, an extraordinary social and psychological phenomenon, has usually tended to encourage group action as if to allay faltering doubts by the sheer weight of numbers.

This spirit has been particularly evident in prayer. Mass praying has been a custom since ancient days. The cynical Petronius (who surely needed prayer) was of the opinion that "Prayers travel more strongly when said in unison."

The worldly Madame de Stael reflected: "To pray together, in whatever tongue or ritual, is the most tender brotherhood of hope and sympathy that men can contract in this life."

To convenience such communal litany organized

churches, from the two main schools of Buddhism to the disciplined ritual of Islam and the unusual variety of Christian sectarianism, have compiled special collections of praying literature.

In Christianity the best known include the *Liturgy of St. James* (Greek), *Liturgy of St. Basil* (Greek), *Liturgy of the Greek Church* (Alexandria, Antioch, and Byzantine rites), *Liturgy of St. Mark* (Greek), *Coptic Liturgy of St. Cyril, Leonine Sacramentary, Gelasian Sacramentary, Gallican Sacramentary, Gregorian Sacramentary, Roman Breviary, Sarum Use* (compiled by the Norman St. Osmund, appointed Bishop of Salisbury by William the Conqueror).

Also the *Mozarabic Rite* (of Spanish origin), *Jacobite Liturgy, Russian Liturgy* (the old Slavonic compendium of St. Basil), and of course, *The Book of Common Prayer* used by the Church of England as its official liturgy, famous for the beauty of its language. This replaced all earlier psalters.

The Book of Common Prayer grew from a luxuriant thicket of litany. Its first complete edition was commissioned by the young King Edward VI and appeared in January 1549. It was, in fact, mainly a direct translation of pre-Reformation Latin services.

Subsequent editions developed their own style and far more poetic language, reflecting the literary ferment that produced the generations of Skelton, Shakespeare, and Donne. Gradually the liturgy grew naturally from the rich vernacular common to seventeenth-century England. This in turn came to accord with the solemn musical language of Handel's lovely fugues.

That the title of Chapter One in my own small anthology derives from a great English Renaissance work is as obvious as it is impertinent. Yet my intention is to widen the scope of prayers, as shown by those herein gathered, remembering that appeals for aid or paeans to beauty need not always be linked to formalized worship.

Indeed, as William Blake warned, sometimes: "As the caterpillar chooses the fairest leaves to lay her eggs on, so the priest lays his curse on the fairest joys." Prejudiced by my atheism, I take the side of Thomas Jefferson, who was not so far as I know an atheist but at least an anticleric.

Jefferson wrote dolefully and angrily:

> In every country and in every age, the priest has been hostile to liberty. He is always in alliance with the despot, abetting his abuses in return for protection to his own.

What I have here called "Deist Prayers" I have so labeled because in one or another way they seem to me to touch, at least lightly, on Deism. By Deism I mean a sense of God's purely mechanical operation upon the universe, a rationalistic doctrine vaguely agreed on the need to construct a natural religion by the light of pure reason, discrediting revelation and thereby, it would seem, faith.

Such logic implies placid acceptance of destiny. It allows for the construction of one's own ethical code, based upon philosophical goodness alone and not upon divine counsel.

Typical is the approach of Tibet's great sage when he grew old in his cave on a wind-swept escarpment looking down upon the world:

> I am of the Josays [descendants of noblemen]
> Sept of the Khyungpo [eagle] Clan, and my own
> personal name is Mila-Repa. In my youth I committed
> some black deeds, in my maturity some white deeds;
> but now I have done away with all distinctions of
> black or white. Having accomplished the chief task,
> I now am one who needeth not strive any more
> in future.
>
> *Yogi Milarepa of Tibet*

One contemporary American poet, perhaps horrified to be included in any anthology remotely religious, expresses a similar spirit of acceptance:

> "yes, yes,
>   that's what
> I wanted,
>   I always wanted,
> I always wanted
>   to return
> to the body
>   where I was born."
>
> *Allen Ginsberg "Howl"*

Is this so far from the Phrygian Stoic's teaching that true education lies in recognizing that only one thing is fully our own—our will or purpose:

> What else can I, a lame old man, do but sing hymns to God? If I were a nightingale I would act the part of a nightingale; if a swan, the part of a swan;

but since I am a reasonable creature, it is my duty
to praise God. This is my business. I do it.

Epictetus

An early Christian father was later to counsel
somewhat similarly:

> Depart from the highway and transplant thyself
> in some inclosed ground; for it is hard for a tree
> which stands by the wayside, to keep her fruit,
> till it be ripe.

St. Chrysostom

The highly moralistic Sikhs, fierce warriors and
proud people, seem to me to share a Deist concept with
the dutiful sense of Epictetus:

> He refused to perform any miracle,
> A cheap way of fooling people.
> Real Prophets of God are ashamed
> Of displaying their occult powers.

*Guru Gobind Singh (last of the ten
Sikh Gurus, 1675–1708)*

As is to be expected, the above spirit of modest
realism resembles much Hindu doctrine, the religious
code from which the Sikh faith originally stemmed:

> From the unreal lead me to the real;
> from darkness lead me to light;
> from death lead me to deathlessness.

Ancient Indian prayer

Off the Pacific coast of the Alaskan mainland
the Tsimshian peoples felt a similar relationship
to the mysteries of nature:

There was a town. One evening a man went out of the
house, and his son accompanied him. They sat down
on the beach. After they had been sitting there for
some time, the boy looked up to the sky and
said to a star, "Poor fellow! You little twinkler,
indeed, you must feel cold." Thus spoke the boy
to the Star. The Star heard it, and one evening
when the boy went out, the Star came down
and took him up to the sky.

Tsimshian Texts

This mood was shared by the greatest symphonic
composer:

Almighty One, in the woods I am blessed.
Happy everyone in the woods. Every tree speaks
through thee.

Beethoven

Far away, on the plateaus of Spain, we find it
echoed by the agonized and holy Juan:

Shepherd, Shepherd, hearing that calling,
Hearken, Hearken, the day is dawning.

St. John of the Cross

And, far distant in time and space, the same idea
fills the valley of the sleepy Nile:

Hail to thee, Ammon Ra, Lord of the
    thrones of the earth, the oldest
        existence,
    ancient of heaven, support of all things;
    Chief of the gods, Lord of truth;
        father of
    the gods, maker of men and beasts and
        herbs;

maker of all things above and below;
    Deliverer of the sufferer and
        oppressed,
judging the poor;
    Lord of wisdom, Lord of mercy;
        most loving,
opener of every eye, source of joy,
    in whose
goodness the gods rejoice, thou whose
    name is hidden.
Thou art the one, maker of all that
    is,
the one; the only one, maker of gods and
    men;
giving food to all.
Hail to thee, thou one with many heads;
sleepless where all others sleep, adoration
    to thee.
Hail to thee from all creatures from
    every
land, from the height of heaven, from the
    depth of the sea.
The spirits thou hast made extol thee,
    saying,
welcome to thee, father of the fathers
    of the gods;
we worship thy spirit which is in us.

"Hymn to Ammon Ra" (Egyptian)

   Nezahualcóyotl, Hungry Wolf, king of the Toltecs
and a splendid poet whose verses were recited at
his command to the accompaniment of conch-shell
trumpets and percussion instruments, who ordered
slain the unfortunate musician who struck a wrong
note, felt he had personally to depend on some
external source for natural tranquility:

These idols of wood and stone can neither hear nor
feel, much less could they make the heavens and the
earth and man the lord of it. Some all-powerful
unknown god is creator of the universe on whom alone
I must rely for consolation and support.

Nezahualcóyotl, Toltec ruler

Loneliness, and dependence on something else,
mark even the doctrines of those resigned to acceptance and who console themselves with rationalism,
a prayer that divinity—even in its abstract form—
will ease the passage through this world:

> O Lord, Embodiment of the Eternal Buddhas,
> Thou Refuge of all Sentient Creatures,
> Out of the depths of Thy Great Love and Wisdom
> Hearest Thou the lamentation of Thy Suppliant
>   Unfortunate,
> Rechung-Dorje-Tagpa?
>
> Unto Thee, in misery and woe, I cry;
> If Thou wilt not Thy Love and Wisdom now exert
> To shield Thy Son, for whom else shouldst Thou,
>   Lord? . . .
>
> Exert Thy Kindness, grant Thy Grace, O Father.

Yogi Milarepa of Tibet

Coleridge, never saintly and frequently befuddled
by the beauties of the opium poppy, saw loveliness
in his relationship even with hateful creatures:

> Beyond the shadow of the ship,
> I watch'd the water-snakes:
> They moved in tracks of shining white
> And when they rear'd, the elfish light
> Fell off in hoary flakes.

Within the shadow of the ship
I watch'd their rich attire:
Blue, glossy green, and velvet black,
They coil'd and swam; and every track
Was a flash of golden fire.

O happy living things! No tongue
Their beauty might declare:
A spring of love gush'd from my heart,
And I bless'd them unaware:
Sure my kind saint took pity on me,
And I bless'd them unaware.

Samuel Taylor Coleridge
"The Rime of the Ancient Mariner"

Animals have a special role in many versions of Deistic thought. The Pacific Indians contemplated them in terms of magic:

Then the great master of the squirrels was glad, because his tribe had come to life again. Then the prince sang: "Iá hēiaha ä, hēia haä′ ayâ nēgwâ'iahâ! I become accustomed to this side; I become accustomed to the other side." He stood there, and was a great shaman.

Tsimshian Texts (Squirrel)

And deep in the Brazilian thickets, along the Gurupi river, southeast of the Amazonian mouth, another unrelated tribe linked divine magic with animalistic creatures:

In the beginning was the Light, there was nothing but the Light, there was only Maira and the Light. Maira created the earth and the great rivers. Then he called the Great Ape and told him to plan the jungle.

Keapor Indian myth

I have often wondered if this simple Indian legend does not contain a profound truth: Was man the Great Ape who proceeded to plan the jungle we today inhabit?

The tenderest of Irish saints (no Deist, he) had a gentle relationship with dumb creatures:

> St. Columcille's old white horse, perceiving that his master was about to die, came and shed tears into his lap. "Let him alone," murmured the saint to those who would have driven the horse away, "for he loves me."
>
> *Irish tale*

And beasts appear as symbols of godhood in the Buddhist sacred literature:

> O Lord, when signs of Thy miraculous siddhi
>   Thou didst show
> Like a lion or an elephant Thou wert,
> A Yogī fearless and strong of spirit;
> To Thee, Thou One Devoid of Fear, we pray:
> Grant to us the Chaitya which the Dakinis now
>   hold,
> To us, Thy Shishyas and Thy Followers on Earth.
>
> *The Nirvāna (Hymn of Entreaty)*

The holiness perceived by those whose thinking (or its expression) I see touched with Deism is always brushed by love, be it carnal or divine. The American poet of the hippy epoch felt this, and his lines are the equivalent of a paean, if not a prayer:

> Holy time in eternity holy eternity in time holy the clocks in space holy the fourth dimension holy the fifth International holy the Angel in Moloch!

Holy the sea holy the desert holy the railroad holy the
    locomotive holy the visions holy the hallucinations
    holy the miracles holy the eyeball holy the abyss!
Holy forgiveness! mercy! charity! faith! Holy! Ours!
    bodies! suffering! magnanimity!
Holy the supernatural extra brilliant intelligent
    kindness of the soul!

Allen Ginsberg

Ishtar, Assyrian precursor of lovely Aphrodite,
born of a fleck of sea foam off the coast of Cyprus,
was a goddess devoted to love as an aspect of religion:

> Come, Gilgamesh, be thou my lover!
> Do but grant me of thy fruit.
> Thou shalt be my husband, and I will be thy wife.
> I will harness for thee a chariot of lapis and gold,
> Whose wheels are gold and whose horns are brass.
> Thou shalt have storm-demons to hitch on for
>   mighty mules.
> In the fragrance of cedars thou shalt enter our
>   house.
> When our house thou enterest,
> Threshold and dais shall kiss thy feet!

Ishtar

And finally, to conclude, again we listen to the voice
of the Buddhist sage, craving but holy relics of the
Supreme Being to confirm, as it were, his existence, and
anyway, to serve as tokens to adore:

> O Lord, when Thou midst many didst preside,
> Thou wert o'erflowing with the milk of sympathy
>   and love,
> And didst save all and set them on the Path,

While those most filled with sorrow Thou didst
    pity specially;
Graciously be pleased to grant to us [a portion of]
    Thy Sacred Reliques,
To serve as objects of veneration and of faith
Unto them who have not zeal and energy [like
    Thine].

Yogi Milarepa of Tibet

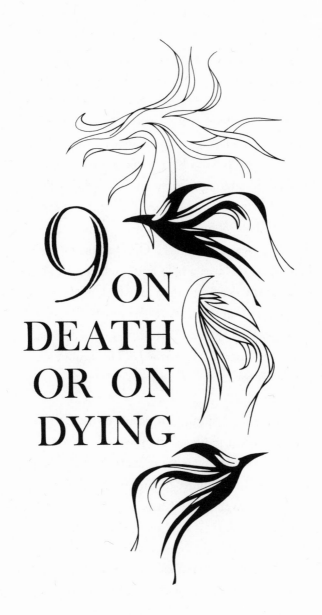

9

ON DEATH OR ON DYING

Most godless persons (like myself) don't pray . . . except when they are frightened. Perhaps they are lazy; faith, after all, requires effort. But for the God-fearing, prayer is an ingrained or imposed discipline, and it is closely related to death and the fear of that condition, a fear which probably started the whole thing off—including religion itself.

Prayers for the dead are as old as any traces of formalized language. They are recounted with pathos in the Egyptian *Book of the Dead* and in the cuneiform relics of Sumeria. Judaism inherited the practice and, as is related in the Old Testament Book of Maccabees II: "It is a holy and a wholesome thing to pray for the dead that they may be loosed from sin."

The tradition was passed on to early Christians, among whose writers Tertullian referred to such ritual as "customary." He warned, "The widow who does not pray for her dead husband has as good as divorced him."

To me the stern implications of formalized religion, so often rendered even less tolerant and forgiving by the preachers of its frequently contradictory sects, tend more to frighten man than give him solace. Even in the Christ legend, suffering Jesus pinioned to the cross (although as divinity he need never have suffered), breaks—also as divinity—under torture and cries: "My God, why hast Thou forsaken me?" Being both Son of God and God himself, the paradox is wholly incomprehensible.

That astonishing genius, Christopher Marlowe, stabbed to death in a brawl, was savagely attacked for heresy when he noted such illogic four centuries ago. As a contemporary chronicler wrote:

> Hee denied God and his sonne Christ, and not only in word blasphemed the trinitie, but also [as it is credibly reported] wrote books against it, affirming our Sauior to be but a deceiuer, and Moses to be but a coniurer and seducer of the people, and the holy Bible to be but vaine and idle stories, and all religion but a deuice of pollicie.

Marlowe was accused of asserting:

> That Crist deserved better to dy then Barrabas and that the Jewes made a good Choise though Barrabas were both a thief and a murtherer. That if there be any god of any good Religion, then it is in the Papistes because the service of god is performed with more Cerimonies, as Elevation of the mass, organs, singing men, Shaven Crownes, & cta.
>
> That all protestantes are Hypocriticall asses. . . . That the first beginning of Religioun was only to keep men in awe.

The final charge, related by another poet-playwright, Thomas Nashe, was that Marlowe asserted the sacraments "would haue bin much better being administered in a Tobacco pipe."

When Marlowe was slain he had no inclination to recant in final prayer. The chronicler tells us:

> The manner of his death being so terrible (for hee euen cursed and blasphemed to the last gaspe, and togither with his breath an oth flew out of his mouth) that it was not only a manifest signe of Gods iudgement, but also an horrible and fearefull terrour to all that beheld him.

There is reason to believe that Marlowe's atheistic speculations were encouraged by the influence of the great Italian philosopher Giordano Bruno, a deeply if heretically religious man. Bruno visited England from 1583 to 1585 while the poet was still at Cambridge University. He became the friend of several Elizabethan intellectuals.

The Italian, burned at the stake, a victim of the Counter-Reformation, is one of the few famous religious thinkers who did not fall back on prayer and ask God for support through his final sufferings. When sentenced by a church court he stood bolt upright from the traditional kneeling position, and he announced to his judges: "Your fears in reading the sentence are perhaps greater than mine in receiving it."

Kepler, the great astronomer, wrote to a friend:

> I hear from Wacker [Johann Matthaeus Wacker von Wachenfelsz] that Bruno was burnt in Rome and that he firmly endured the torture, maintaining that all religions are vain and that God is to be identified with the world, with the circle, and with the point.

Bruno's conception—and when he died for it, he had no illusion that blissful eternity awaited him elsewhere—has been pondered along similar lines by later thinkers, both theist and atheist. J. B. S. Haldane, the twentieth-century British scientist, mused (as already mentioned earlier): "The universe is not only queerer than we suppose but queerer than we *can* suppose."

This analysis cannot escape theological conclusions.

A disordered universe—or series of universes—negates the ordered concept, with shape, beginning, and end, on which the original idea of divinity was postulated: the Creator of what had not previously existed, the survivor after doomsday.

Now, led by the astronomers and their spatial black holes, we find with T. S. Eliot (himself a believing High Churchman): "They all go into dark, The dark vacant interstellar spaces, the vacant into the vacant."

Such, for me, is death, the topic of these entreaties and prayers.

One subject about which we have learned nothing, absolutely nothing, despite the vast explosion of knowledge touched off by human intelligence during its brief reign on earth, is death. We do not truly know what it means or where it leads. We abhor its corruption. We have no genuine confidence that it implies any form of transmogrification which contains within itself a germ of life, even a new and unfamiliar version of life.

Faith has been invented as a crutch to help us along the inevitable journey into the unknown, whence nothing, no one, has ever returned or sent a message of instruction. And for those who cannot hypnotize their minds into a condition of faith, immutable death means immutable destruction. It is the kingdom of the underworld described by the Phoenician god Baal:

> . . . his city Ruin,
> Dilapidation is the throne on which he sits,
> Loathesomeness is the land of his inheritance.
>
> *The Baal Myth (Baal's embassy to*
> *Mot, lord of the underworld)*

The ancient Egyptians both revered and feared
death and they greeted its arrival with lovely poetry
and infinite pathos:

> According to native Egyptian accounts, which
> supplement that of Plutarch, when Isis had found the
> corpse of her husband Osiris, she and her sister
> Nephthys sat down beside it and uttered a lament
> which in after ages became the type of all Egyptian
> lamentations for the dead. "Come to thy house," they
> wailed. "Come to thy house. O god On! Come to thy
> house, thou who hast no foes. O fair youth, come to
> thy house, that thou mayest see me."
>
> *"The Golden Bough," Frazer*

Throughout time every man, if he could think at
all, has thought of death even though, for curious
sociological reasons, it has not been regarded as a fit
matter for written or spoken discussion since the
seventeenth century. Then, indeed, it was chic.

There is a gentle and philosophical, weary acceptance of death's reality in many religions. I knew
the head of the heretical Islamic sect of Bektashi in
Albania almost forty years ago, and used to discuss
both life and death with him and his monks at the
order's *tekke* in the mountain town of Kruja. He
counseled:

Tolerance is what is important. And death, as a brother, comes to embrace all men.

Grand Baba of the Islamic Order of the Bektashi

Death undoubtedly is often a welcome state to the sick, the weary, the disconsolate. Indeed, those in such sad straits often actively seek its embrace. For, as we are reminded by the great Greek dramatist:

> O Death the Healer,
> scorn thou not, I pray,
> To come to me: of cureless ills thou art
> The one physician. Pain lays not its touch
> Upon a corpse.
>
> *Aeschylus*

Indeed, as Malraux tells us in *Lazare,* there is no reason why a man should not, in extremis, kill himself. He writes:

> What is written on suicide has always surprised me. The absurd need to turn it into a fault, or a merit. Born to die, man is born to take his own life if he so decides.

And we are counseled by the learned simply not to think of death; there are better things to contemplate, as it were:

> A free man thinks of death least of all things; and wisdom is a meditation not of death but of life.
>
> *Spinoza*

Surely a generous spirit is grateful for the opportunity to exist and therefore to contemplate death,

which is preferable after all to total nonexistence,
the state of being eternally unborn, of never having
had opportunity to contemplate the exquisite joys and
sorrows of life, brief as it is:

> You wish that I leave this magnificent spectacle, I leave
> it; and I thank You a thousand times over that You
> have deigned to admit me there where I can see Your
> works manifested and to see before my eyes the order
> with which You govern this universe.
>
> *Epictetus*

A Babylonian epic hero said the obvious as well
as any man and sooner than most:

> Only the gods live forever under the sun.
> As for mankind, numbered are their days;
> Whatever they achieve is but wind!
> Even here thou art afraid of death.
> What of thy heroic might?
>
> *Gilgamesh*

And, as is so often the case, the earlier and unknown Egyptian poet bewailed it yet more poig-
nantly:

> Death is before me today as the odor of myrrh. . . .
> Death is before me today as the odor of lotus
> flowers. . . . Say not: "I am too young for thee to
> carry off," for thou knowest not thy death.
>
> *Book of the Dead*

The great Central American poet-ruler, whose
work has been preserved for us by Spanish friars who
accompanied the conquistadores, had a magnificent

view of death's sepulcher amid the panorama of the heavens:

> All things on earth have their term, and in the most joyous career of their vanity and splendor, their strength fails, and they sink into the dust. All the round world is but a sepulcher; and there is nothing, which lives on its surface, which shall not be hidden and entombed beneath it. Rivers, torrents, and streams move onward to their destination. Not one flows back to its pleasant source. . . .
>
> The great, the wise, the valiant, the beautiful—alas! where are they now? They are all mingled with the clod; and that which has befallen them shall happen to us, and to those that come after us.
>
> Yet let us take courage, illustrious nobles and chieftains, true friends and loyal subjects, let us aspire to that heaven where all is eternal, and corruption cannot come. The horrors of the tomb are but the cradle of the sun, and the dark shadows of death are brilliant lights for the stars.

> *Nezahualcóyotl, King of the Toltecs*

Many Oriental philosophers and priests see death only as a cessation of striving, once a human has accompanied the task his brief life was designed for. The Hindu epics put this conception in a frightening way:

> This transitory life resembles a man pursued by a raging elephant. And it cornered him inside a fearsome abyss. Then he caught sight of some trees onto which he climbed and then saw two mice, one black and one white, which were gnawing away the roots of the trees up which the man had clambered. And he looked down into the chasm and noticed a dragon, which had parted

its jaws and was intent on swallowing him. And he looked up above and saw a little honey trickling down the trees, and he began to lick it up. And now he remembered no longer the peril into which he had fallen. But the mice gnawed through the trees, and the man fell down, and the elephant seized him and hurled him over to the dragon. Now, O king's son, that elephant is the image of death, which pursues the sons of men; and the trees this transitory existence; and the mice are the days and nights; and the honey is the sweetness of the passing world; and the savor of the passing world diverts mankind. So the days and nights are accomplished and death seizes him and the dragon swallows him down into hell; and this is the life of men.

Balahvar

The great Kha-Khan, fiercest conqueror of all time, accepted his end with philosophical tranquility, advising the stinking warriors gathered about him in his felt tent on the windy heartland steppes:

Do not make a lament or raise a clamor about my death, for such things do no good; never yet has death been frightened away by screaming. Instead of rending your garments and running hither and thither like lunatics, pray God to be gracious to me; say prayers that will delight my soul.

Genghis Khan

Despite his fierce depredations, including, in one Afghan valley where his son was slain, the destruction of each living thing, every blade of grass, Genghis seemingly died without fear and with what others call a clear conscience. Such was not the case with another Asian ravager, the Great Mogul. As he lay expiring, he said:

After me the chaos. I came a stranger to this world
and a stranger I depart.

> *Emperor Aurungzeb, the Great Mogul*
> *(before dying at the age of ninety)*

Then, as death seized him, he still had the strength
to murmur:

I am so evil that I fear God will have no place for me.
Therefore bury me bareheaded, for they say that all
those who come bareheaded into God's presence will
receive His mercy. But I do not believe He will dare to
look at me.

> *Emperor Aurungzeb (dying)*

One who accepted death with the same equanimity
he showed to life was the wise sage of the storm-
swept Himalayas who, regarding humanity from the
world's rooftop, counseled:

Hold your peace and no litigation will arise;
Maintain the State of Undistractedness and
distraction will fly off;
Dwell alone and ye shall find a friend;
Take the lowest place and ye shall reach the
highest;
Hasten slowly and ye shall soon arrive;
Renounce all worldly goals and ye shall reach
the highest goal.

(Thus did Jetsün pass away at the age of eighty-four
years, on the fourteenth day of the last of the three
winter months of the Wood-Hare Year [A.D. 1135],
at dawn.)

> *Yogi Milarepa of Tibet*

The mighty Gilgamesh acknowledged that naught

was known of death, including its duration, which
remained a mystery:

> Do they not compose a picture of death,
> The commoner and the noble,
> Once they are near to their fate.
> The Anunnaki, the great gods, foregather;
> Mammetum, maker of fate, with them the fate
>   decrees:
> Death and life they determine,
> But of death, its days are not revealed.
>
> *Gilgamesh*

And the finest among modern poets of that race
of bards, the Welsh, protested fiercely against death
(to no avail, alas):

> And you, my father, there on the sad height,
> Curse, bless, me now with your fierce tears, I pray.
> Do not go gentle into that good night.
> Rage, rage against the dying of the light.
>
> *Dylan Thomas*

Euripides had a remarkably conventional and
acute approach to man's relationship with his end,
saying with sad cynicism:

> Old men's prayers for death are lying prayers, in which
> they abuse old age and long extent of life. But when
> death draws near, not one is willing to die, and age
> no longer is a burden to them.
>
> *Euripides*

But most prayers on the subject tend to accommodate
to its inevitability and request divine aid in preparing
for the tomb. Thus (in this case optimistically):

> Teach me to live, that I may dread
> The grave as little as my bed;
> Teach me to die, that so I may
> Rise glorious at the awful day.

> *Bishop Thomas Ken*

Lord Byron, the swashbuckling romantic poet, was no great praying man, and yet his expressed desire echoes that of Bishop Ken, the hymnologist:

> And, since I soon must cease to live,
> Instruct me how to die.

> *Lord Byron*

In the seventeenth century, when men had no shame in discussing death, and were fascinated to depict it and describe it, the great dean of St. Paul's scared the wits out of more-timorous members of his congregation by reminding them:

> After my skin my body shall be destroyed. Though not destroyed by being resolved to ashes in the fire (perchance I shall not be burnt), not destroyed by being washed to slime, in the sea (perchance I shall not be drowned), but destroyed contemptibly, by those whom I breed and feed, by worms.

> *John Donne*

But his contemporary, a fellow writer and adored idol of most fishermen, was far more cheerful on this favorite subject of his time. He wrote:

> With this or the former, I have often suspected myself to be overtaken, which is, with an overearnest desire of the next life. And though I know it is not merely a

weariness of this, because I had the same desire when I went with the tide, and enjoyed fairer hopes than I now do.

Isaak Walton

And the courageous, stern old rebel against Roman rule in Palestine, in a most modern way discerned a form of immortality in man's actions and the legacy of glory left behind:

> Now at this time there was one whose name was Mattathias, who dwelt at Modin, the son of John, the son of Simeon, the son of Asamoneus, a priest of the order of Joarib, and a citizen of Jerusalem. . . .
>
> When he had ruled one year, and was fallen into a distemper, he called for his sons, and set them round about him, and said, "O my sons, I am going the way of all the earth, and I recommend to you my resolution, and beseech you not to be negligent in keeping it. . . . Your bodies are mortal, and subject to fate, but they receive a sort of immortality, by the remembrance of what actions they have done. And I would have you so in love with this immortality, that you may pursue after glory, and that, when you have undergone the greatest difficulties, you may not scruple, for such things, to lose your lives. . . ."

Flavius Josephus

Because death is so powerfully linked with religion and therefore with prayer, it is the single subject that most inspires mankind to authorship, either oral or written, of at least a few words, a phrase, a plea. Thus the brave warrior, otherwise unknown to history:

> Here lies Luka Vladosavić. I was a bold hero. I

beseech you, brothers, disturb not my bones. You will be as I am, but I cannot be as you are.

Bogomil tombstone near
Dubrovnik, Yugoslavia

The canonized saints, not surprisingly, approach death with tranquility and confidence:

O good Shepherd, seek me out, and bring me home to Thy fold again. Deal favorably with me according to Thy good pleasure, till I may dwell in Thy house all the days of my life, and praise Thee for ever and ever with them that are there.

St. Jerome

And with astounding indifference to pain a legion of martyrs has welcomed the cold relief of death:

Lord, they tear my body, receive Thou my soul [and the faithful followed behind sopping up his blood in sponges as his body was rent by wild horses].

St. Hippolytus

At the moment of dying an extraordinary number of men and women, both good and evil, have uttered last words which are almost always specifically couched in the form of prayer. Accordingly:

O my Lord, the hour I have so much longed for has surely come at last. The time has surely come that we shall see one another. My Lord and Savior, it is surely time for me to be taken out of this banishment and be forever with Thee. The sacrifices of God are a broken spirit, a broken and a contrite heart, O God, Thou wilt not despise. . . . Cast me not away from Thy presence, and take in me a clean heart, O God. . . . A broken and a contrite heart Thou will not despise.

St. Teresa of Avila (dying)

Sometimes the word "prayer" is used only in the form of an urgent request, like that of a noble lady about to be beheaded:

> I pray thee carry a message from me that I die a true woman of my religion, like a true Queen of Scotland and France. But God forgive them that have long desired my end and thirsted for my blood, as the hart does for the water-brooks. Commend me to my dearest and most sweet son [the future King James I]. Tell him I have done nothing to prejudice him in his realm, nor to disparage his dignity.
>
> *Mary, Queen of Scots*

Or in another instance (again, "I pray"), that of a patriotic officer of his country hanged by the cruel custom of war but ultimately removed to a shrine in London's Westminster Abbey. By Washington's order, the Continentals executed the British spy Major André at Tappan in 1780. Says the journal of Dr. Thacher, Revolutionary surgeon in attendance:

> It was his earnest desire to be shot, as being the mode of death most conformable to the feelings of a military man, and he had indulged the hope that his request would be granted. . . . Col. Scammel now informed him that he had an opportunity to speak, if he desired it. He raised the handkerchief from his eyes, and said, 'I pray you to bear me witness that I met my fate like a brave man.' The wagon being now removed from under him, he was suspended and instantly expired. . . .
>
> *Thacher's* Journal

The stern and God-fearing Lord Protector of the realm of Britain gave a brusque pardon to future generations and spoke with the curt paucity of a military man when, on his bed of death, he turned to God:

> Pardon such as desire to trample upon the dust of a poor worm, for they are Thy People too. And pardon the folly of this short Prayer: —even for Jesus Christ's sake. And give us a good night, if it be thy pleasure. AMEN.

> *Oliver Cromwell*

Another strong English soul, that of a woman, was filled with compassion for her fellow humans when she stood before a firing squad amid the cold October Belgian mud:

> I have no fear or shrinking. I have seen death so often that it is not strange or fearful to me. . . . But this I would say, standing as I do in view of God and eternity: I realize that patriotism is not enough. I must have no hatred or bitterness toward any one.

> *Nurse Edith Cavell (shot in 1915 by the Germans in occupied Belgium)*

Those who have been executed by the sword and fire have often on occasion, despite their bravery, prayed for assistance to a swift end. So a great fourteenth-century peer spoke:

> So popular was his execution that it had to be postponed for a day owing to the enormous crowds blocking the way to the scaffold. Nothing could have been more exemplary than his end: "Strike thrice," he bade the headsman, "for the honor of the Trinity."

> *John Tiptoft, Earl of Worcester*

And when a renowned English pair of martyrs addressed each other amid the flames, it was with the exquisite passion of pain:

> Latimer: Be of good comfort, Master Ridley, and play the man. We shall this day light such a candle, by God's grace, in England, as I trust shall never be put out.

> Ridley: Let the fire come unto me, I cannot burn.

Hugh Latimer and Nicholas Ridley

How haunting, that doubtful prayer of a virtuous young Arab beauty, graven upon her Maltese tomb:

> Alas, death has robbed me of my short life; neither my piety nor my modesty could save me from him. I was industrious in my work, and all that I did is reckoned and remains.

> Oh, thou who lookest upon this grave in which I am enclosed, dust has covered my eyelids and the corners of my eyes.

> On my couch and in my abode there is nought but tears; and what will happen when my Creator comes to me?

Tombstone of Maimuna, daughter of Hassan (on the island of Gozo, Malta)

Some people (and they are not many) hasten through life impatiently in order to achieve its mysterious final goal:

> Lord, I am coming as fast as I can. I know I must pass through the shadow of death, before I can come to Thee.

Archbishop Laud

Others, without rushing toward death, perceive it from the very first instant of conscious thought:

> We have a winding-sheet in our mother's womb . . . and we come into the world wound up in that winding-sheet; for we come to seek a grave. . . . We celebrate our funeral with cries, even at our birth.
>
> *John Donne*

And there are even some who see in the grave's tranquility a strange improvement over the turmoil of life, of continually choosing and striving to exist:

> Didst Thou forget that man prefers peace, and even death, to freedom of choice in the knowledge of good and evil?
>
> *Feodor Dostoevski*

Here are some memorable last words that come from the smug satisfaction of a man who was fully proud that he had lived right, and on his deathbed was equally determined to die right:

> Wife, children, doctor, I trust on this occasion I have said nothing unworthy of Daniel Webster.
>
> *Daniel Webster*

And what can be finer than this appeal to his divinity, Allah, by that medieval Kurdish mystic who prayed only:

> O Lord, may the end of my life be the best of it,
> May my closing acts be my best acts,
> And make the best of my days the day when I
>   shall meet Thee.
>
> *Abd al Qadir al Jilani* (A.D. *1166*)

During our time, who can have lived a purer or a more effective life, who could have been readier for any form of death, than saintly Mohandas Gandhi, diminutive, ascetic, arrogantly modest, and already seventy-eight years old? This century's greatest soul (and most original politician) told a New Delhi prayer meeting on January 15, 1948, fifteen days before his murder:

> He who is born in this world cannot escape death. . . . Death is a great friend to all. It is always worthy of our gratitude, because it relieves us of all sorts of miseries once and for all.

Six days later he said:

> What better death could you ask than to die in the act of prayer?

On the day of his assassination by Hindu extremists he sang (with his followers) this verse from the Bhagavad Gita:

> For certain is death for the born and certain is
>   birth for the dead;
> Therefore over the inevitable
> Thou shouldst not grieve.

That same evening, shot three times, he murmured his final words: *"He Ram!"* [Oh God] . . . and expired.

10 L'ENVOI

All my life, despite my refusal of religion, I have been fascinated by and respectful of the reverence it inspires. I have collected its prayers and enjoyed its ceremonials, some of which include man's most touching and most glorious creations. Through these aspects of a craving for divinity, so common to humanity, I have come with that gallant soul, Sir Walter Raleigh, to believe that "Our life is but a wandering to find a home," although, unlike that courteous Elizabethan, the home I look forward to is nothingness. But what of that? Why should that inspire distress? Did not Homer tell us so many aeons ago:

> Come my friend you must die.
>> What tears can help your need?
> Patroclus also is dead a better man far than you.
> See what a man am I, strong of body and fair to
>> view.
> A kindly father begot me. I was born of a goddess's
>> womb,
> But over me too stand death and overmastering
>> doom. . . .

For many years I have had a house on a Greek island where I have spent some of my most agreeable moments with (at various times) five generations of my family, and there I once wrote a book called *My Brother Death,* with whose final words I close this gentle anthology in my own kind of prayer:

> Now, come, my Brother Death; now, old, old, old, with hair like thistledown, I sink with fatigue into the soft Aegean waters that bear me northward and backward into time.

ACKNOWLEDGMENTS

Once again I want to thank Isabel Bass and Linda Lamarche for their help in preparing this book, and my wife Marina for her wise, critical observations.

It is impossible to give proper acknowledgment for republication of these excerpts of prayers to all publishers of books which contained them; I have culled this material in scraps and bits over forty years and have no adequate records—so I *pray* the tolerance of all good publishers, let them not complain.

I do, however, wish to make a special mention of my gratitude to that remarkable sourcebook, the *Encyclopaedia Britannica,* for some of its analysis of prayers, praying, their history and meaning.

INDEX

Note: Page references to quotations are in *italics*.